# BEAUTY AND THE LAW

A Primer in Philosophy and Theology for Enquiring
Minds Committed to the Common Good

*Based upon four lectures delivered at the*
*Lawyers' Christian Fellowship Annual Conference,*
*Rydal Hall, Cumbria, United Kingdom, June 2024*

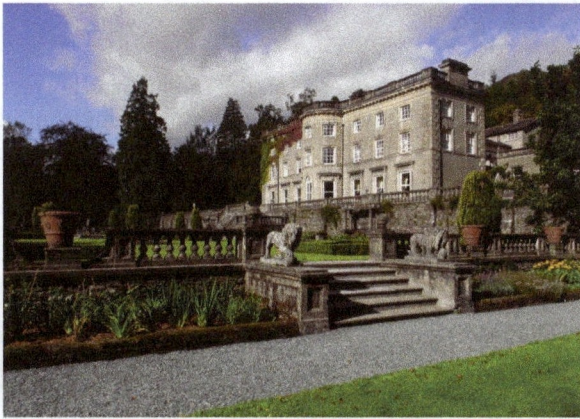

## Dr Mark Fowler

Adjunct Associate Professor at the University of Notre Dame,
School of Law, Sydney

Adjunct Associate Professor in the Law School at the University of
New England

External Fellow at the Centre for Public, International and
Comparative Law, University of Queensland

### Foreword

The Hon Ian DF Callinan AC

Brent Haywood

**Shepherd Street Press**

Published in 2024 by Connor Court Publishing Pty Ltd under the imprint Shepherd Street Press.

Shepherd Street Press is an imprint of Connor Court Publishing and the School of Law, The University of Notre Dame Australia, Broadway.

Copyright © Mark Fowler

Connor Court Publishing Pty Ltd

PO Box 7257

Redland Bay QLD 4165

sales@connorcourt.com

www.connorcourt.com

Phone: 0497-900-685

ISBN: 9781923224438

Cover Design by Ian James

Cover illustration: Michael Galovic, *The Timeless Dance Triptych*, 2016, 120 x 120cm

Printed in Australia.

*For Caitlyn and Ethan*

'Law, say the gardeners, is the sun'
WH Auden, *Law Like Love*

# CONTENTS

# ACKNOWLEDGEMENTS

From its first conception, *Beauty and the Law* has been a collaborative effort, for which many expressions of thanks are owed. First to Jesus Christ, author and perfecter of the faith. Second, to my wife Sarah, without whose love and support this project would not have been completed. Thanks are owed to various persons who commented on earlier drafts of the book, or otherwise were influential in its formation, including Dr Richard and Judy Thornton, Reverend Canon Dr Rhys Bezzant, Professor Nicholas Aroney, Thomas Eglinton, Dr Matthew Turnour, Drs Matthew and Emily Best, Ben Fullbrook, Professor Keith Thompson and Professor Iain Benson. Especial thanks go to Mark Bainbridge whose request to deliver this lecture series afforded the justification to take time out of a busy legal practice and the prompting to compose this book. I am also indebted to the various attendees at the Lawyers' Christian Fellowship 2024 annual conference who provided their reflections on these lectures, and by whose comments they have been vastly improved. My gratitude is also owed to Justice Patrick Keane AC KC for offering to launch the book, and also to Karen Fowler, Professor Michael Quinlan, Dr Lorraine Finlay, Aaron Alexander, Nicholas Churchill, Iain Sutherland, Michael Galovic, Stella Loong, Anthony Cappello, Michael Gilchrist, Graydon Burgess and Thor Mula who also encouraged the creation of this work in their various ways.

# FOREWORD FROM AUSTRALIA

Nothing could be more apt for the times than the publication of Dr Fowler's original and insightful lectures about Western Civilisation, its learnings, traditions and essential contributions to society and the laws to govern it. Dr Fowler makes a strong case for the enduring relevance of these and Christianity as an integral part of them.

Dr Fowler weaves throughout his argument various thought-provoking illustrations drawn from his own experiences in the practice of law, including amongst Australian and South-East Asian indigenous communities. There is much with which to agree in the United Nations Declaration of the Rights of Indigenous People adopted by the General Assembly of the United of Nation on the 13th of September 2007. Among other things that august body seeks to uphold by the Declaration the cultures of Indigenous Peoples wherever born or living.

As recent as 2007 is, one would not have thought that any provision would need to be made for the protection or promotion of the values of Christianity and Western Civilisation. But to the impartial observer, the contrary often appears to be the case, an example of which is the rejection by the majority of Australian universities of a generous endowment by the late Paul Ramsay AO via the Ramsay foundation of a chair for the teaching of Western Civilisation.

Nor would the impartial observer have thought it necessary for there to be any special measures for the protection of people of the Christian faith but again the current debate regarding legislation for a federal human rights law would suggest otherwise.

Dr Fowler's elegantly constructed lectures drawing upon history, law, literature, the Bible and the Constitution itself deal at a philosophical and practical level with these paradoxes in an increasingly secular age. This anthology is not however written exclusively for the philosopher or the lawyer. It is enlivened by poetry, parable and anecdote.

This reader was taken by the story of the drafting of the Australian Constitution which Dr Fowler rightly sees as unique and a thing of beauty in itself. During the cruise on the Hawkesbury by the founders of this nation, at one point those far-minded men went ashore and some of them chose to bathe under a natural waterfall on the river or one of its tributaries. Dr Fowler has read all of the important documents relating to the composition of the Constitution, including an account of that bathing party by Sir Samuel Griffith who apparently chose not to refresh himself under that stream.

Beauty and the Law could not be more relevant than it is today. It is to be commended to everyone.

**The Hon Ian Callinan AC KC**

# Foreword from the United Kingdom

Thirty-five years ago I was presented before the High Court of New Zealand as a new barrister and solicitor. I was sworn in by a presiding judge who emphasised that I was entering a vocation. During the window of my time in the law in both New Zealand and Scotland I have witnessed a profession challenged by commoditisation and the notion that it is merely the seller of legal services. Now we face the implications of Artificial Intelligence, where might that take us?

During the summer of 2024 it was my privilege to be present in the English Lake District when Mark Fowler delivered to the Lawyers' Christian Fellowship this series of four lectures on 'Beauty and the Law'. With forensic clarity these lectures unlock the connectedness between truth, goodness, and beauty in a way which refreshed this battle-scared litigator's passion to creatively promote justice in a flawed, yet functioning, legal system.

By shining both philosophical and biblical teaching on beauty into the shadows of postmodernity Mark Fowler provides an opportunity to look reflectively at truth, justice, and law. He challenges the lawyer to see the essential link between divine beauty and justice and to embrace the weaving of these concepts into an artistry that can be a springboard to genuine creative lawyering in whatever field of the law we inhabit.

This work concludes with a prescient critique into the polity of today. Applying what we have learnt on the journey Fowler asks, 'can there be a Christian Political Philosophy?' Read and see if you agree.

May these lectures on beauty inspire your creative contribution to the law as you work with clients, colleagues, courts or constitutions.

**Brent Haywood**
**Solicitor Advocate – Edinburgh**

# ENDORSEMENTS

'If beauty can light up pathways to human flourishing, we are greatly indebted to Mark Fowler for helping us find the switch again, so long lost in the gloom of our blind materialism.'

**The Hon John Anderson, former Deputy Prime Minister of Australia**

\* \* \*

'Of the three classical transcendentals, truth, goodness and beauty, it is the latter that is perhaps the least understood. Beauty can seem remote to the nature and practice of the law. Mark Fowler shows, drawing on history, theology, literature, art and philosophy, that beauty as the pursuit of justice is at the very heart of law-making, advocacy and judicial decision making. And importantly, he demonstrates the danger that postmodern notions of relativism present to the hopeful and charitable character of the project of western civilization because of its dependence on the enduring appreciation of the true, the good and the beautiful.'

**The Hon Amanda Stoker, former Commonwealth Assistant Attorney-General**

\* \* \*

'In the post-modern world our understanding of beauty is focused on the superficial. Mark Fowler encourages us to explore a more consequential understanding by examining the inextricable connection between beauty, truth and the good. Seeing the beauty within our fellow man is a reminder of our common humanity. Seeing the beauty within the law allows us to look beyond rules and order, and search instead for justice. This book is a timely reminder that beauty is not a shallow construct but has a much deeper significance for the individual human soul and the broader human condition.'

**Commissioner Lorraine Finlay, Australian Human Rights Commissioner**

'Beauty has become a leading category of communication in our age, whether we are talking about art, personal morality, sports, or even the law. And no wonder, for it captures our aspirations for harmony, wholeness, and well-being. Mark Fowler has done us a great service in these lectures to draw our attention to the divine gift of beauty, and its relevance to the public sphere. Let's continue to advocate for its power.'

**Reverend Canon Dr Rhys Bezzant, Principal (elect), Ridley College, Melbourne**

\* \* \*

'This useful volume relates two concepts, justice and beauty, not often held together in contemporary thinking. A dominant philosophy called "positivism" rests too confidently on a supposed inseparable divide between all disciplines (including law) and morality. Yet justice is a virtue and, as a virtue, depends upon a certain relation to the foundations of natural law: cosmos, human reason, human nature, metaphysics and education itself. Dr Fowler does a great job of reminding us that law, to be justice, must be related to matters beyond mere law itself and that beauty and what it relates to is one of these important informing notions. A much needed book.'

**Iain T Benson, Professor of Law, University of Notre Dame Australia, Sydney**

# PREFACE

This book is written for those who wish to make a contribution to the common good through their labour in the workplace. It is intended as an introduction for the time-poor professional to the resources of philosophy (including aesthetics, metaphysics, epistemology, theodicy and political philosophy) and theology. It was originally conceived as a series of lectures provided at the Lawyers' Christian Fellowship Annual Conference held at Rydal Hall, Cumbria, United Kingdom, June 2024. While the audience for the original lectures was comprised of Christian lawyers, all those who seek a sense of vocation within their work will take benefit from this book. It will also be a resource to those wishing to attain to a greater understanding of the relation between religion, philosophy and jurisprudence.

The book is not intended to deliver a comprehensive account of the intellectual history of the West, but instead to introduce time-poor professionals to various of the resources of philosophy and the Christian tradition that are relevant to their vocations. Its treatment of many centuries of enquiry by the some of the greatest minds within the Western tradition is necessarily curt. It will likely leave the practicing philosopher with the sense of having sat down to an insubstantial meal; some may be decidedly irked. Some will no doubt legitimately question the choices I have made in directing the readers' attention toward certain philosophers and theologians over others. You are not my audience. Rather, it is hoped that this short primer will inspire, or further, a life-long love of philosophical and theological enquiry for the reader whose interest is first piqued. For that enquirer, further resources are listed in the bibliography.

Although the original lectures have been expanded upon, including in the light of the generous reflections of those in attendance, I have retained various of the original references to localities within Cumbria for their capacity to illustrate the themes encountered. The questions used for group discussion at the conference following each successive lecture are included at the conclusion of each chapter. They are intended for use by discussion groups that adopt this book as a framework for their own enquiry.

# LECTURE 1

## *She has Done a Beautiful Thing*

### Introduction

We cannot aspire to an accurate understanding of Western civilisation without understanding its treatment of 'beauty'. From antiquity the claim has been made that there is a relation between the 'true', the 'good' and the 'beautiful'. Plato's vision of the just society realised the deep relation between these three 'transcendentals'; where 'the true' (that which defines ultimate reality), 'the good' (that which fulfills its purpose or *telos*) and 'the beautiful' (that which is lovely) achieve practical coherence. In his 1970 Nobel Prize in Literature acceptance speech Solzhenitsyn claimed that the burden of communicating the relation between truth, the good and beauty fell uniquely upon the artist: 'all that is given to the artist is to have a keener sense than others of the world's harmony and of the beauty and ugliness of man's contribution to it, and to convey this vividly to others.'[1] From within Soviet Russia Solzhenitsyn declared his unwavering faith in art, and particularly literature, as unrelenting preserves of truth and as windows into the eternal: '[y]ou look into it and you glimpse – not yourself: you glimpse for an instant the Inaccessible, whither you can never gallop or fly. And only a deep yearning remains.'[2]

CS Lewis similarly sought to highlight the power of beauty to direct our attention to eternal truth and the eternal good; to cause us to 'notice' our 'spiritual longing'. Reflecting on that which Keats called 'the journey homeward to habitual self',[3] Lewis writes: 'as the

---

[1] Aleksandr Solzhenitsyn, 'Nobel Lecture in Literature 1970' *Letter to The Swedish Academy*, 1970, tr Michael Scammell 12 <https://journals.sagepub.com/doi/pdf/10.1177/030642207200103-402> The lecture was not given, owing to Solzhenitsyn's effective confinement in the Soviet Union, and is thus not dated. It was instead delivered by letter to The Swedish Academy.

[2] Ibid 13.

[3] John Keats, 'Endymion', *The Complete Poems of Shelley and Keats* (Random House, 1978) 75, 2.76.

moment of vision dies away, as the music ends or as the landscape loses the celestial light' we realise that '[f]or a few minutes we have had the illusion of belonging to that world' of the eternal.[4] The same awareness of beauty's power to open a fleeting glimpse of the eternal is found in these verses from TS Eliot's *The Dry Salvages*:

> the winter lightning
> Or the waterfall, or music heard so deeply
> That it is not heard at all ...
> These are only hints and guesses,
> Hints followed by guesses; and the rest
> Is prayer, observance, discipline, thought and action.[5]

However, in our own time the classical relation between beauty, truth and the good has been thrown akilter; or perhaps more than akilter, we might say it has been thrown aside. In this series of four lectures, originally delivered to an audience of lawyers in the beautiful setting of the Cumbrian lakes district, I will contend that our society's current post-modern malaise is a direct consequence of this development. I will explore the extent to which we might see correspondence between the role of the artist and that of the lawyer. In so doing, I adopt the term 'lawyer' as a broad signifier to encompass not only the solicitor, advocate, barrister, the legislator and policy-maker, but all who would wish to more completely direct their professional labours to the common good. I will develop an argument that conceives of the lawyer (so described) in the service of *beauty*, understood as *justice*, and as a central protagonist in the reply to the problem of evil, and postmodernism. We will consider how an understanding of history, particularly intellectual history, may make us architects by informing our contribution to the common good. We will search for a unifying theoretical framework for the lawyer who senses their well-meaning contributions to the common good

---

[4]  CS Lewis, *The Weight of Glory and Other Addresses* (The Macmillan Company, 1949) 11.

[5]  TS Eliot, 'The Dry Salvages', *The Four Quartets* (Faber & Faber, 2019) 41.

to be all-too inchoate or haphazard. Drawing upon the deep wells of Western intellectual history and of Christian theology, we will consider whether we may locate a political philosophy that is sufficient to enable a lawyer's action toward the common good within the state in which liberalism has assumed ascendency.

## The *Australian Constitution* – A Study in How Beauty Might Inspire Creative Legal Thinking

We commence our journey into beauty and the law with a reflection from Australian Constitutional history. The 1891 draft of the *Australian Constitution* was finished not far from my home, on the Hawkesbury River, just north of Sydney. My interest toward this event was piqued as I have some small purchase in the Hawkesbury, where I have had the recent pleasure of learning to sail with my boy. The Constitutional drafters had set out from Port Jackson on Easter Friday 1891 onboard the *Lucinda*, a Queensland government steamer on which Sir Samuel Griffith had travelled from Brisbane. The intent was, as La Nauze describes it, to get away from reporters to a place 'where [the vessel] could lie in peace in the beautiful waters of the estuary of the Hawkesbury River.'[6] Barton described the Lucinda's anchorage at 'a most lovely place called Refuge Bay' replete with a bush waterfall providing a natural showerbath, which Sir Samuel Griffith conceded 'I did not take it myself' (the implication being that others did).[7] Bolton tells us that '[t]hroughout Friday evening, Saturday and Sunday morning the drafting party laboured intensively in the gentlemen's smoking-room in the upper fore-cabin.'[8] Of the resulting product La Nauze would say: 'the draft of 1891 is

---

[6] JA La Nauze, *The Making of the Australian Constitution* (Melbourne University Press, 1972) 65. See also James Edelman, 'Original Constitutional Lessons: Marriage, Defence, Juries, and Aliens' (2021) 47(3) *Monash University Law Review* 1; Bernhard Ringrose Wise, *The Making of the Australian Commonwealth 1889-1900: A Stage in the Growth of the Empire* (Longmans, Green, and Co, 1913); Geoffrey Bolton, *Edmund Barton* (Allen & Unwin, 2000).

[7] Bolton (n 6) 79.

[8] La Nauze (n 6) 80.

the Constitution of 1900, not its father or grandfather.'[9] Bernhard Wise, at the time a thirty-three year old former New South Wales Attorney-General, would later write:

> It may be explained, at this distance of time, by one who assisted at this conclave unofficially, that the occasional missing of the happiest turn of phrase by these distinguished draftsmen may have been due to the sea-sickness, which followed the surreptitious heading of the steamer out to sea, and the rise of a wind before she could return to harbour![10]

Notwithstanding, it seems that the solitude of this beautiful setting was not without effect. La Nauze writes that '[a]s English prose, appropriate for its dignified yet technical purpose, the evolving text of the Constitution was at its best after the *Lucinda* revisions.'[11]

So we make take some confidence that beauty can inspire creative legal drafting; for we may even have beauty to thank for the felicitous language of the *Australian Constitution*. But beauty's legal effect goes beyond its potential to inspire the deft turn of the drafter's pen. Indeed, only around the river bend from Refuge Bay at Milsons Island, a sanatorium was built on the premise that the beautiful setting would assist the rehabilitation of returning World War One soldiers with 'shell shock'. This gives us hope that we lawyers are correct in coming with the expectation of our own respite and creative inspiration amidst the tranquil setting of the Cumbrian lakes, far removed from the stress-inducing life of adrenaline we are habituated to. In the immediacy of practice our attention is kept continually on such practical questions as 'what is the best outcome for my client?', or 'who caused this detriment?' We scarcely find time to consider the questions of 'why?': 'why was it I chose a career in the law?', or 'what': 'to what end did I chose it?' Moreover, even if we enjoy some vague sense of having set out on the adventure of law to

---

[9]  Ibid 78.

[10]  Wise (n 6) 126.

[11]  La Nauze (n 6) 66.

contribute to the common weal, we rarely find the time, or perhaps desire, to reflect on the further question: 'what would be the most efficacious use of my time toward that end?'

The fast pace of the modern workplace rarely affords opportunity for the gathering of perspective. Each individual client, file or matter bears little coherence to the preceding. Can you discern a unifying narrative mapping the arc of trajectory across the differing retainers with which you have been engaged, or is there simply none to be found? Legal practice affords precious little time to ask these hard questions. And yet, if our contribution to the common good is to last, we will require a unifying narrative sufficient to motivate and rationalise our many disparate efforts, and to bear the weight of opposition to those efforts. In these lectures I will adopt the phrase 'causa agendi' as a descriptor for the unifying narrative that we seek. In Roman law the causa agendi was the 'cause of action' in a court of law. In Roman jurisprudence a 'causa' could also refer to a motive, intention or purpose underpinning one's behaviour. 'Agendi' means 'of action', to act in fulfilment of that which needs to be done. The literal translation of causa agendi is the meaning that I have in view in these lectures: *that motivation which causes us to do what needs to be done.* Theoretical coherence in one's causa agendi is the fruit that can only follow the blessing of uninterrupted contemplation, afforded to us over this weekend together. The age-old contest between the 'contemplative' and the 'active life', and the hope of the 'composite'[12] of the two, has great salience for the lawyer. After all, as Augustine said, if we were 'obliged wholly to relinquish the sweets of contemplation … the burden might prove more than we could bear.'[13]

## The History of Beauty in the West

In this serene setting I am aspiring to offer you a panoramic view of the contemporary Christian lawyer's emplacement within (fol-

---

[12] Augustine, 'City of God' in Robert Maynard Hutchins (ed), *Great Books of the Western World: Augustine* (Encyclopaedia Brittanica, 1952) 523, bk 19, ch 19.

[13] Ibid.

lowing Nietzsche) a genealogy of Western intellectual history.[14] The
history of the West is the history of the dynamic tradition famously
coined by Tertullian when he asked in the third-century: '[w]hat
then has Athens to do with Jerusalem, or the Academy with the
Church?'[15] As Daniel Mahoney summarises, these two great traditions present the 'dialectic of magnanimity and humility [which]
has marked the West from the beginning and continues to operate within our liberal dispensation.'[16] The philosopher Leo Strauss,
also following Nietzsche, emphasised that 'this unresolved conflict
[between the two traditions] is the secret of the vitality of Western
civilisation',[17] for 'we must be aware of the fact that the vitality and
the glory of our Western tradition are inseparable from its problematic character.'[18] Noting this, I want to start out on our journey
together through beauty and the law by considering the unique
contributions these two great traditions have made to our Western
understanding of beauty.

## Athens – The Priority of Harmony

Let us then commence with Athens. Within the Greek tradition
beauty was inextricably linked to the notion of harmony, where the
idea of beauty as 'unity in variety' took prominence. In the *Metaphysics* Aristotle asserted that the 'chief forms of beauty are order
and symmetry and definiteness'.[19] Aristotle's teacher Plato located
beauty in the realm of his transcendental Forms. The beauty of

---

[14]   Friedrich Nietzsche, *Beyond Good and Evil*, tr Walter Kaufmann (Vintage
Books, 1966) 3, 100-2, 211; Friedrich Nietzsche, *The Genealogy of Morals*, tr
Horace B Samuel (Dover Publications Inc, 2003) 24-5.

[15]   Tertullian, 'De Praescriptione Haereticorum' 7(34), 9 quoted in Edwin Judge,
*Jerusalem and Athens* (Mohr Siebeck, 2010) vi.

[16]   Daniel J Mahoney, 'Communion and Consent' (2012) 41(2) *Perspectives on
Political Science* 93, 96.

[17]   Leo Strauss, 'Progress or Return?' (1981) 1(1) *Modern Judaism* 17, 44.

[18]   Leo Strauss, 'Thucydides' 72 quoted in John Ranieri, 'Leo Strauss on Jerusalem and Athens' (2002) 22(2) *Shofar* 85, 88.

[19]   Aristotle, 'Metaphysics' in Robert Maynard Hutchins (ed), *Great Books of the
Western World: Aristotle I*, tr WD Ross (Encyclopaedia Brittanica, 1952) 610,
1078a36-1078b1.

objects was found in their participation in the Forms, which were themselves in an elaborate harmonious relation with the Good. The classical notion of beauty as the harmony of proportion also made its way into Greek political philosophy. Plato's theoretical just society was a community in ultimate coherence with objective reality; coherent with the three transcendentals 'the true', 'the good' and 'the beautiful'. To better assure that coherence, his Republic was to be presided over by philosophers as Kings, harmonising conflicting human interests so to instantiate the good as the common good.[20] Notably for our current investigation, Plato held that meditation on the beautiful could lead one 'to contemplate and see the beauty of laws and institutions'.[21] At the very foundations of Western political philosophy we thus find a striking assertion of the direct relation between beauty and the law.

## Jerusalem – 'She Has Done a Beautiful Thing'

The association of beauty with harmony was also found within the second great pillar definitive of Western civilisation, the tradition of 'Jerusalem'. As NT Wright tells us:

> The word beauty doesn't occur much in the Bible, but the celebration of creation all the way from Genesis, through the Psalms and Prophets, on into the gospels and here in Revelation, should alert us to the fact that, though the ancient Jewish people did not theorize about beauty like the Greeks did … they knew a great deal about it and poured their rich aesthetic sensibility not only into poetry but also into one building in particular: the temple in Jerusalem, whose legendary beauty inspired poets, musicians, and dancers alike.[22]

---

[20] Plato, 'The Republic' in Robert Maynard Hutchins (ed), *Great Books of the Western World: The Dialogues of Plato*, tr Benjamin Jowett (Encyclopaedia Brittanica, 1952).

[21] Plato, 'Symposium' in Robert Maynard Hutchins (ed), *Great Books of the Western World: The Dialogues of Plato* tr Benjamin Jowett (Encyclopaedia Brittanica, 1952) 167, §210.

[22] NT Wright, *On Earth as in Heaven* (HarperOne, 2022) 40-1.

God's choice of the Old Testament Temple as His place of residence on earth and His care and attention to its elaborate design and adornments speak to the great worth He places upon material beauty. The Temple narrative tells us that the God of the Bible's glory seeks, resides within, and is synonymous with, beauty. Wright reminds us '[t]hat great vision [of the nations entering the heavenly Temple] at the end of the book of Revelation is a vision of ultimate beauty.'[23] In that vision the beauty of the resting place of God welcomes in the beauty offered by the nations, where '[t]he glory and honor of the nations will be brought into it.'[24] We are thus presented with the tri-fold affirmation that the Biblical God's eternal glory is synonymous with beauty; that humans may produce and offer beauty; and that His beauty seeks to join with our own created beauty. If we were to apply the Greek notions of the true and the good to this eschatological vision, we might say that, as He instantiates both the true and the good, the relation of these two with beauty is completed in Him. The offering to Him of our own beauty presents our acceptance of the relation between the three.

One of the few occasions in which the translators of the New International Version of the Bible tell us that Jesus engages with the concept of 'beauty' is in the phrase 'she has done a beautiful thing to me', appearing at Mark 14:6 and Matthew 26:10. Jesus utters the phrase in response to the unsolicited pouring of 'very expensive perfume' on his body 'to prepare for [his] burial'.[25] The Greek term for beauty deployed by Jesus (καλός) bears the notion that He considers the woman's act to be in pleasant alignment with what is eternally fitting and good for that precise moment. We might see a degree of correspondence between Jesus' sense of beauty as being that which is in coherence with the eternally fitting and the Platonic notion of

---

[23] Ibid.

[24] *The Holy Bible: New International Version*, (Biblica, 2011) Revelation 21:26. 'The glory and honor of the nations will be brought into it.' Unless otherwise indicated, in this book Biblical references are taken from *The Holy Bible: New International Version*, (Biblica, 2011).

[25] Mark 14:3, 8.

the harmonious interaction of truth, the good and beauty. Whether Jesus intended this or not, to my mind the correspondence with the Greek understanding of the interaction of beauty, truth and the good is unmistakable. (However, notwithstanding this correspondence, which Augustine also noted,[26] we must be cautious to not strain credulity by overlooking the many deep distinctions between the two traditions of Jerusalem and Athens.[27])

This is not the only place in the Bible in which we find the assertion that that which is in harmony with God's will is beautiful. In Jeremiah 18:13-15 the Lord describes Israel's rejection of Him as being synonymous with a rupture of the harmonious beauty of nature:

Therefore this is what the Lord says:

"Inquire among the nations:
Who has ever heard anything like this?
A most horrible thing has been done by Virgin Israel.
Does the snow of Lebanon
ever vanish from its rocky slopes?
Do its cool waters from distant sources
ever stop flowing?
Yet my people have forgotten me ..."

For God's beloved people to 'forget' Him is as unnatural to divine order, as *unbeautiful*, as snow vanishing from its natural habitat and mountain rivers ceasing to fall. Here the natural is beauty and sin is unnatural; the extinguishment of beauty. Here, mutual loving relationship between God and His people is as natural and as beautiful as the snow and cool waters of Lebanon's mountain scapes. We see this same correspondence in Hosea 2:21-22, where God's response to the discordant incursion of Israel's sin is to promise the restoration of harmony in eternity. Again that unity is pointedly signified by

---

[26] Augustine (n 12) 267, bk 8, ch 5.

[27] See, eg, Marc BieMiller, 'Augustine and Plato: Clarifying Misconceptions' 29(2) *Aporia* 33; John Peter Kenney, '"None Come Closer to Us than These:" Augustine and the Platonists' (2016) 7(9) *Religions* 114.

a vision of nature as beauty, this time in harmonic correspondence with Him and His people: "'In that day I will respond," declares the LORD— "I will respond to the skies, and they will respond to the earth; and the earth will respond to the grain, the new wine and the olive oil, and they will respond to Jezreel'. Isaiah extends the metaphor of unity expressed through the beauteous harmony of nature in his famous description of the eschaton, where 'the mountains and hills will burst into song before you, and all the trees of the field will clap their hands.'[28]

## Christianity to the Enlightenment

The next stage in this very high-level journey through the development of 'beauty' within Western civilisation is the movement from Christendom to the Enlightenment. Christianity drew deeply on the preceding Jewish and Greek understanding of beauty as harmony. This influence is evidenced, for example, in Augustine's 391 AD claim that '[i]n all the arts, that which pleases is harmony, which... invests the whole [of a work] with unity and beauty, either through the resemblance of symmetrical parts, or through the graded arrangement of unequal parts'.[29] The Judeo-Christian understanding of beauty prevailed relatively unassailed until the eighteenth century, when it was to find itself in sharp conflict with a new contender: Enlightenment philosophy. To illustrate the substance and depth of that conflict it is first necessary to set out some certain basic elements of the Judeo-Christian account of beauty. I will offer you four illustrations demonstrating how the Biblical conception of nature and of humanity as created works leads to the Christian understanding of the necessity of beauty to human fulfilment. Having laid that framework we will be positioned to consider the depth of the challenge presented to that understanding of beauty by the Enlightenment reason of the eighteenth century onward.

---

[28] Isaiah 55:12.
[29] Augustine *De Vera Religione* quoted in James Gallant, 'What am I Doing?' (2023) 153 *Philosophy Now* 19, 19.

First, in placing Adam and Eve in the serene setting of the Garden of Eden, God from the very outset set our need for beauty at the essence of that which constitutes the human. It is no mistake that the Bible pointedly confirms that the Garden was 'pleasing to the eye'; to our visual senses.[30] God in His wisdom created humanity as physical beings able to appreciate, indeed not only able, but *needing* to appreciate the beauty of the surroundings in which He placed us. That God would place us in an aesthetically pleasing setting as our 'original position'[31] would suggest to us that an appreciation of natural beauty is necessary to the proper fulfilment of our human condition. How fitting that we sit together tonight right next to 'Britain's earliest known purpose-built viewing station' recognising this necessity.[32] The affectionately named 'Grot' was constructed by Sir Daniel Fleming in 1668 to enable enjoyment of the serene view of the waterfall next to Rydal Hall.

*'The Grot', Rydal Hall, Cumbria, United Kingdom*

---

[30] Genesis 2:9.

[31] John Rawls, *A Theory of Justice* (Belknap Press, rev ed, 1999). This is a whimsical reference in comparative terminology. I am not intending to equate John Rawls' account of the original position to the Biblical account of the Garden of Eden.

[32] Placard inscription at the site of the Grot.

Therefore, according to the Biblical account, we may take some confidence that, in arriving in the serene setting of the Cumbrian lakes district, we harried and debilitated lawyers, habituated to the constrictive four walls of our urban environment, have rightly come to enjoy nature in fulfilment of our own nature.

Second, as we saw with the account of the Old Testament Temple's design and adornments, beauty can reside in settings outside of nature and also in material objects. We would be forlornly mistaken were we to think that we are obligated to escape the dense metropolis if we are to encounter beauty. Solzhenitsyn cherished beauty precisely for its irrepressibility. In its persistence it will invade our daily work lives, if we retain eyes to see it and ears to hear it. This offers great hope to the busy professional. The Biblical understanding that we created beings require beauty to fulfil our humanity explains why we find our encounter with beauty to be replenishing. Much like 'sweet friendship', beauty is marked by its ability to 'refresh the soul and awaken our hearts with joy'.[33] For the beleaguered city worker maintaining an expectation of its tenacious, unpredictable upwelling can be a lifeline.

Surveying just my limited city surrounds, beauty has made herself known in the delicate alignment of architraves in the sandstone Cathedral nearby to my office; in various works of street art and fountains; in the bustling excitement of a stretch of cafés framed under an avenue of leopard trees; in worn steps leading into arched, mysteriously inviting laneways; in the heritage-listed Bulimba wharf; in the Opera House's animated curves.[34] It has made itself known through non-material means, in the lunch-time visits from my wife and infant children; in the joy of my colleagues in seeing

---

[33] *The Holy Bible: The Passion Translation* (Broadstreet Publishing Group, 2020) https://www.thepassiontranslation.com/read-online/ Proverbs 27:9.

[34] The website of Street Level Australia Inc, a body devoted to 'the advancement of culture by promoting excellence and beauty in design through the mediums of architecture, urban design and the building arts', offers an excellent introduction for those interested in the pursuit of beauty within our urban environment. See www.streetlevelaustralia.org.

them; and in the monthly student classical music recital held in a nearby church. The over-abundance of beauty found in nature also invades even the city. I have found it in the sunset over the river as I make my commute home; in the familiar remembrance inspired by the spectrum of light that casts across my desk at the same time each year as the trajectory of the sun disperses through an imperceptible incline in my window. I have found it in the sonorous calls of the Currawongs refracting off the Brisbane skyscrapers that arrest me in my rush to the bus stop after the summer sunset rains. Although hidden in the avenues of leopard trees out of sight, their calls became like an old friend coming to refresh my soul at the end of a heavy day. Such encounters with beauty are necessary to the human condition. We office workers do well to take the time to heed them when they encroach uninvited into our busy lives. We do well to savour their ability to refresh our spirits. In so doing we provide them permission to, as Lewis has it, cause us to 'notice' our 'spiritual longing' amid our busy lives.[35] Beauty is not the sole preserve of sublime settings such as that in which we currently find ourselves here in Cumbria. It is laced throughout the creation, and even the metropolis will not prevail against it.

Third, the Bible's creation account also speaks of the necessity of beauty to the human condition in its description of the relation between humanity and the animal kingdom. After creating the plant kingdom as 'pleasing to the eye'[36] and the animal kingdom as 'good', God creates Adam and Eve 'in his own image',[37] and commissions them to 'take care of' the creation.[38] Am I correct to have always read a certain eager expectation on the part of God within the text 'He brought the [animals] to the man to see what he would name them'?[39] The fact that God was interested in our reflections on what

---

[35] Lewis (n 4) 11.

[36] Genesis 2:9.

[37] Genesis 1:22, 27.

[38] Genesis 2:15.

[39] Genesis 2:19.

He considers to be 'good' suggests to me His desire for dialogue with us in matters of beauty. God seeks our enjoyment in what is 'good', in this case His creativity expressed in the animal kingdom. In a world where God enjoyed 'walking in the garden in the cool of the day',[40] the creation account gives us a clear sense of God's desire to enjoy *with us* that which is beautiful in His creatures. In God's pursuit of our reflections upon the animals, the text suggests that our relationship with those creatures is itself beautiful. In Isaiah's famous vision of the heavenly Jerusalem we are presented with the culmination of this relationship, one akin to that first enjoyed in the Garden:

> The wolf will live with the lamb,
>     the leopard will lie down with the goat,
> the calf and the lion and the yearling together;
>     and a little child will lead them …
> The infant will play near the cobra's den,
>     and the young child will put its hand into the viper's nest.[41]

If you will permit me a personal reflection, that God's intention that we experience the beauty of nature in our relationship with the animal kingdom has persisted this side of the Fall has been brought home to me in recent years through the purchase of a horse. For me, there is something unparalleled in horse riding; in traversing rough terrain the rider's and the horse's sensate perception and awareness come into close alignment. In my experience, if you get a good horse, the enjoyment of the ride is reciprocated between rider and horse. Evidence of the much cited 'bond' between master and horse is found in the anticipation of the horse toward its time with its master. This is but one example of a tangible relation with the animal kingdom gifted to us by God, a further illustration of the necessity of beauty to the fulfilment of our human condition.

The beauty of our relationship with the animal kingdom was again brought home to me in a recent visit to the Malaysian Nation-

---

[40] Genesis 3:8.
[41] Isaiah 11:6, 8.

al Zoo accompanied by one of the resident keepers, my old friend Herman. My ten-year-old boy was simply captivated by Herman's relationship with the animals. At the sound of his call, the young giraffe he had reared by hand meandered across the enclave with curious expectation; an enormous crocodile arose to the surface from the dark of its pool; and a colossal aged and swarthy elephant strode over to us. In enjoying my young son's ever-growing delight across the day it occurred to me that Herman's relationships with the animals were anything but abnormal. Instead, they seemed to bring to completion that which is proper to humankind, that which is natural. They struck me as an opening, a strange crack of light through to what was originally intended for humanity in relation to creation. The point I am pressing is that the unique and unchartable relation between man and beast falls within the manifold ways that God intended creation fulfil our need for beauty.

The final illustration in this exploration of how God has made beauty necessary to the human condition according to the Biblical account is found in the capacity of beauty to be enhanced in enjoyment when experienced with other human beings. Notice that He placed Adam and Eve in the Garden to enjoy its beauty *together*. Notice also that the act of worship in the beauty of the Old Testament Temple was a *corporate* act. God made us to enjoy beauty as human beings *together*. When I was confident that my son and I were finally sufficiently proficient in the use of our sailboat for my wife Sarah to join us, I could scarcely contain my excitement. The day had finally come in which I could show her the beauty of the Hawkesbury River by boat. The expectation of her enjoying this with Ethan and I, of diving into cool waters to explore a remote island she had never been to, with my boy leading; of returning to dock with the surrounding sandstone cliffs ablaze with the late-afternoon light, these were the delightful thoughts I savoured for weeks in advance of the big day, which did not ultimately disappoint.

A similar encounter with the capacity of beauty to be enhanced through its shared enjoyment occurred when we as a family recently bundled into a Ferris Wheel cab together. The physical experience of height, of the swaying movement and of scrambling for the limited cover to escape the unexpected downpour of rain had us brimming with shared expectation, excitement and plain old-fashioned laughter and joy. However, I felt strongly for the dear child in the next cab, who provided a much-contrasted picture sitting by herself as her family watched and waited for her on the ground below. Not only is beauty fundamental to the fulfilment of our human nature, but we are also *geared*, as a fundament of that *nature,* to experience it *together*. Mutuality enhances our experience of beauty; it creates further beauty found in the shared joy of its experience. As Mark Twain has said: 'To get the full value of a joy you must have someone to divide it with'. In the third of these lectures we will return to explore the implications of this thought for professional work and the assertion that it is more fulfilling when it is conducted together with others.

The myriad encounters with beauty across these four illustrations remind us that, according to the creation account, God chose to create us as a mixture of spirit and of material, (loosely) what Enlightenment philosophy would later identify as a combination of 'subject' and 'object'. We are placed in a physical world that God intends we encounter in our physical selves - in a world that God pointedly tells us, in case we should miss it, is created with elements that are 'pleasing to the eye'. This is a Scriptural direction: He has created us to enjoy pleasant sensory experience, to enjoy beauty. Through the Biblical account of creation and the narrative of the beauty of the Old Testament Temple God tells us of the worth he places upon material beauty; that delight in the relation between the observing subject and the observed beautiful object is a fundamental and natural aspect of our human condition.

## The Problem of the Absolute and the Subject/Object Distinction

These illustrations of God's intention that we experience beauty in order to fulfil our own nature agitates one of the key conundrums of

Western philosophy: the subject/object problematic, also sometimes understood as the problem of our relation to 'the absolute'. John Milbank tells us that the subject/object distinction has its origins in the invention of the secular which commenced with the voluntarism of the fourteenth century theologian John Duns Scotus, and his conception of God as pure power separate and apart from His secularised creation, *etsi Deus non daretur* (as if God did not exist). Milbank writes that 'late-medieval nominalism, the Protestant Reformation and seventeenth-century Augustinianism ... completely privatized, spiritualized and transcendalised the sacred'.[42] Drawing upon these roots, Immanuel Kant, following the empirical scepticism of his predecessors John Locke (on the account of Joseph de Maistre[43]) and David Hume, laid a further key foundation of the Enlightenment's secularisation thesis when he posited an epistemology that denied any human access to ultimate reality. Kant held that the *world for us*, the world that humans perceive and conceive through our mental categories and interests (our subjective experience), is entirely distinct from the *world as it is*, ultimate reality independent of the observing subject (the objective world, what he termed the world of 'noumena'; and that which is sometimes known as 'the transcendent' or 'the absolute').[44] The implications of the subject/object distinction for the classical relation of beauty, truth and the good are immediately apparent. If objective reality is unknowable, for what purpose do we seek beauty, the good or truth? To what rational purpose do we seek to align our subjective lives with an objective truth that is simply inscrutable?

---

[42] John Milbank, *Theology and Social Theory* (Blackwell Publishing, 2nd ed, 2006) 9.

[43] Joseph de Maistre, *St Petersburg Dialogues*, tr Richard Lebrun (McGill-Queen's University Press, 1993) 187. See also Pierre Manent, *The City of Man*, tr Marc A LePain (Princeton University Press, 1998) 127; Pierre Manent, *An Intellectual History of Liberalism*, tr Rebecca Balinksi (Princeton University Press, 1995) 7.

[44] See, eg, Immanuel Kant, 'The Critique of Pure Reason', in Robert Maynard Hutchins (ed), *Great Books of the Western World: Kant* tr JMD Meiklejohn (Encyclopedia Brittanica, 1952) 10, Preface to the Second Edition, 1787.

Although it took some considerable time to bear its full fruit, the subject/object distinction has fundamentally altered the Western citizen's way of viewing the world. It also finds expression within the core dispute of the modern philosophy of aesthetics: is an object beautiful because we see beauty in it (the subjective argument), or is it intrinsically beautiful, regardless of any value we ascribe to it (the objective argument). The key question here is: 'does beauty exist outside of our ascription to it?' If it does not, why did my two year old daughter's eyes widen with her breathtaking amazement when first seeing the Brisbane city and river ablaze with sunset light? Why since 1668 have so many come to this Cumbrian estate to sit in 'the Grot' and enjoy the sublime beauty of the waterfall it looks upon? As CS Lewis wrote:

> Until quite modern times all teachers and even all men believed the universe to be such that certain emotional reactions on our part could be either congruous or incongruous to it—believed, in fact, that objects did not merely receive, but could merit, our approval or disapproval, our reverence or our contempt. The reason why Coleridge agreed with the tourist who called the cataract sublime and disagreed with the one who called it pretty was of course that he believed inanimate nature to be such that certain responses could be more 'just' or 'ordinate' or 'appropriate' to it than others. And he believed (correctly) that the tourists thought the same. The man who called the cataract sublime was not intending simply to describe his own emotions about it: he was also claiming that the object was one which merited those emotions.[45]

Beauty's claim to universalism directs our attention to the impli-

---

[45]  CS Lewis, *The Abolition of Man* (The Macmillan Company, 1947) 9-10. Although Samuel Taylor Coleridge toured Cumbria with his friend William Wordsworth in 1797, the incident that Lewis speaks of occurred in Scotland: Dorothy Wordsworth, *Recollections of a Tour Made in Scotland, 1803* (Yale University Press, 1997) 62-5.

cations of the subject/object problematic for the classical relation between beauty, truth and the good. Her claims invite the question: if beauty does not exist outside of our ascription to it, why then not truth also, why then not the good also?

## An Illustration from Indigenous Societies

To explore just how radical the Enlightenment distinction between subject and object is, let me take you on a quick journey through my years in indigenous societies in Borneo and Australia. These societies retain a way of being that considers the material world to be imbued with spiritual meaning, and indeed with its own life. It is a world in which the Enlightenment distinction between subject and object is, at best, a vapid curiosity, at worst, a dangerous deception. As a young man straight out of law school living in these communities I was struck by the indigenous peoples' awareness of the reality of the spiritual domain; it was the medium in which they lived and moved. They experienced this spiritual mode of being in the mendacious spirits in the trees, those appearing at the window or on the veranda of the long house, the mystical ancestors in the waterfall. To this day the witch doctors remain the subject of genuine fear.

I recall a Saturday afternoon in the Aboriginal community when around fifteen Toyota troop carriers drove in carrying indigenous men who had come for what is termed 'payback' for an injury incurred by one of their youth in a fight. These 'troupies', as they are locally known, were surrounded by around 300 locals, armed with baseball bats, bottles and any other makeshift weaponry they could find. In the middle of this scene Kenneth, the indigenous worship pastor, was convicted that we needed to fall to our knees to pray for peace. At the sight of the Christians in this posture of prayer the troupies turned around and left, without any of their modern-day warriors having disembarked. They were, I surmise from other dealings, perhaps either concerned about the harmful effect that our prayer would wreak upon them, or they were concerned that a sacred act was occurring for which they had no initiation into knowledge, and so could not remain. These indigenous people are mystified by the apparent reality in which we secular Westerners understand ourselves to live. They do not comprehend the vacation of the spiritual dimension purportedly effected by the West's secular revolution. I suspect that they do not have the epistemological foundations necessary to truly understand our post-Enlightenment way of conceiving of the world; just as we have lost the foundations to fully comprehend theirs. The complete divorce of the material from the spiritual, of the object from the subject, the imperceptible *animus* from which our Western agency proceeds, is an unfathomable mystery to them.

## The Reply of the Romantics

However, the secular revolution has not in all respects prevailed within our own culture. In their recoil from William Blake's 'dark Satanic mills',[46] the eighteenth and nineteenth Romantics thirsted for a restoration of communication between the material and the spiritual. Their instinctive reaction to the void of the Enlightenment's bleak secularism was to seek the reunification of the subject and the object. In so doing they extended the Christian understanding of beauty as being necessary to the fulfilment of the human condition, albeit (for many among their company) unmoored from its grounding as an intended design of the Biblical God. Having accepted Enlightenment Reason's eschewal of the Christian understanding of the communication between subject and object, the Romantics sought this renewed spirituality through a connection with our materiality within nature. When William Wordsworth wrote *I Wandered Lonely as a Cloud* in these very Cumbrian hills, he was expressing the Romantics' revulsion against the industrial revolution's effect on the human condition. He was also expressing Romanticism's reaction against the Enlightenment's eschewal

---

[46] William Blake, 'And Did Those Feet' in Margaret Ferguson, Mary Jo Salter and Jon Stallworthy (eds), *The Norton Anthology of Poetry* (WW Norton, 5th ed, 2005) 746.

of our spiritual selves in favour of our reasoned selves. So when Wordsworth encounters daffodils he personifies them as a 'crowd', 'a jocund company'. They aren't just swaying in the breeze, they are '[f]luttering and dancing in the breeze', '[t]ossing their heads in sprightly dance'. Even '[t]he waves beside them danced'. In these verses Wordsworth proclaims a reunification between the object and subject, for their dance long after 'flash[es] upon that inward eye' whereupon 'then my heart with pleasure fills, And dances with the daffodils.' Here, Wordsworth stakes a claim in epistemology: the subjective sense of his 'inward eye' is conjoined with the objective beauty of the natural world. In similar defiance of the Enlightenment's deification of reason, John Keats proclaims in *Lamia* that natural science will 'unweave a rainbow'.[47] For Keats the answer lay in our return to the classical transcendentals: '"Beauty is truth, truth beauty,"- that is all Ye know on earth, and all ye need to know.'[48]

The Romantics defiantly proclaim that the Enlightenment separation between material and spiritual, between object and subject, has not altogether prevailed. For them, the experience of beauty *is* the avenue of reclamation. The beauty of nature and of the sublime play a central role in this retrieval effort. That role is clearly evident when Wordsworth writes:

> It is a beauteous evening, calm and free,
> The holy time is quiet as a Nun
> Breathless with adoration; the broad sun
> Is sinking down in its tranquillity;
> The gentleness of heaven broods o'er the Sea;
> Listen! the mighty Being is awake,
> And doth with his eternal motion make
> A sound like thunder—everlastingly.
> Dear child! dear Girl! that walkest with me here,

---

[47] Keats, 'Lamia' (n 3) 155.

[48] Keats, 'Ode On a Grecian Urn' (n 3) 186.

If thou appear untouched by solemn thought,

Thy nature is not therefore less divine:

Thou liest in Abraham's bosom all the year;

And worshipp'st at the Temple's inner shrine,

God being with thee when we know it not.[49]

As the late Roger Scruton has said: 'In the Romantic landscape the beautiful replaces the sacred as the source of meaning.'[50] For the Romantics, as Wordsworth classically shows, the beautiful *is* the sacred.

However, the Romantics were far from the first to make a claim to the sacral character of natural beauty. As Scruton observes, 'land and landscape have been portrayed as sacred in all our human attempts to belong in the world.'[51] As we have seen, for indigenous societies the natural is permeated with the spiritual. The need to imbue the natural with the sacred is also evidenced in the near-mythic quality that the Hawkesbury River assumes for Australian constitutional conservatives today, for the reasons of its emplacement within our history that I articulated earlier. As CS Lewis has shown, according to the Biblical account, natural beauty might be sacred in so far as it might cause us to 'notice' our 'spiritual longing' for the ultimate source of beauty - its Creator.[52] Chesterton elaborates upon the Biblical understanding that creation points us to the need for our Creator when he writes:

> One of the deepest and strangest of all human moods is
> the mood which will suddenly strike us perhaps in a gar-
> den at night, or deep in sloping meadows, the feeling that
> every flower and leaf has uttered something stupendously
> direct and important, and that we have by a prodigy of

---

[49]   William Wordsworth, 'It Is a Beauteous Evening' in Margaret Ferguson, Mary Jo Salter and Jon Stallworthy (eds), *The Norton Anthology of Poetry* (WW Norton, 5th ed, 2005) 794-5.

[50]   Roger Scruton, *The Face of God: The Gifford Lectures* (Bloomsbury Publishing Plc, 2014) 135.

[51]   Ibid 118.

[52]   Lewis, *The Weight of Glory and Other Addresses* (n 4) 11.

imbecility not heard or understood it. There is a certain poetic value, and that a genuine one, in this sense having missed the full meaning of things. There is beauty, not only in wisdom, but in this dazed and dramatic ignorance.[53]

Scruton can be understood to draw these many threads together when he claims that 'the emotion that attaches human subjects to their sacred places is their deepest intimation of what it means to be in the world, and in dialogue with it.'[54] This thought accords with the Biblical understanding that our human nature is fulfilled by our appreciation of the beauty of creation. In the ability to communicate with our material world, to experience the communications that it makes to us, Scruton sees a unique human 'willingness to find meanings and reasons, even in things that have no eyes to look … and no mouth to speak.'[55] Here Scruton makes a claim to the singular role beauty experienced as sacred place plays in collapsing the distinction between subject and object. He argues that:

> The sense of beauty puts a brake upon destruction, by representing its object as irreplaceable. When the world looks back at me with my eyes, as it does in aesthetic experience, it is also addressing me in another way. Something is being revealed to me, and I am being made to stand still and absorb it. It is of course nonsense to suggest that there are naiads in the trees and dryads in the groves. What is revealed to me in the experience of beauty is a fundamental truth about being – the truth that being is a gift, and receiving it is a task.[56]

Expressing a similar hope in beauty, the Romantics' core assumption was that art and the sublime would transcend the Kantian disconnection between the world as we perceive it and the world as it is.

---

[53] Kevin Belmonte, *The Quotable Chesterton: The Wit and Wisdom of GK Chesterton* (Thomas Nelson, 2011) 21.
[54] Scruton (n 50) 118.
[55] Ibid 128.
[56] Ibid 151-2.

In so doing they placed beauty at the centre of the response to postmodernism. Why? Because, as I will argue, Kant's separation of subject from object, in extending Locke's earlier empirical scepticism, is
the intellectual progenitor of contemporary postmodernism.

## Postmodernism

The 'diverse and eclectic' movement that is post-modernism is defined by its 'assumption that there is no common denominator – in
"nature" or "truth" or "God" or "the future" – that guarantees either
the Oneness of the world or the possibility of neutral or objective
thought.'[57] Postmodernism's response to the classical claim that there
is a relation between beauty, truth and the good is succinctly put
by Nietzsche: 'It is unworthy of a philosopher to say that the good
and the beautiful are one, if he goes so far as to say "and also the
true", we should thrash him.'[58] Notwithstanding Nietzsche's claims
to originality, postmodernism's moral relativism is distinctly lacking
in novelty. In the fifth Century before Christ Protagoras theorised
that: 'Man ... is the measure of all things, of the existence of things
that are, and of the non-existence of things that are not.'[59] Be that as
it may, the history of artistic beauty in the West bears much fruit for
the enquirer seeking the origins of the present-day culmination of
our intellectual history in postmodernism. The insight offered by
aesthetics follows from its core inquiry: 'when we apply aesthetic
value to an object is our subjective appreciation purely a matter of
personal taste or is it the appreciation of a substance that itself par-
ticipates in a higher, objective form of beauty?' The postmodern
notion that 'beauty is in the eye of the beholder' is a phrase first
attributed to Margaret Wolfe Hungerford in her 1878 novel *Molly
Bawn*. It is an idea that has a distinct intellectual progenitor in Kant's
separation of subject from object, and his refusal to admit that the

---

[57] Elizabeth Ermath, 'Postmodernism', *Concise Routledge Encyclopaedia of Philosophy* (Routledge, 2000) 700.
[58] Friedrich Nietzsche, *The Will to Power*, tr R Kevin Hill and Michael A Scarpatti (Penguin Books, 2017) 465, §822.
[59] Plato, 'Theaetetus' (n 20) 517, [152a].

*world for us* (our subjective sense) can ever reflect the *world as it is in essence* (objective reality).

We can trace the development of these ideas through the history of art. The Renaissance artist Michaelangelo famously said '[t]he sculpture is already complete within the marble block, before I start my work. It is already there, I just have to chisel away the superfluous material.' Michaelangelo conceives of the task of the Renaissance artist, like the Platonic philosopher, as being to identify the true Form of beauty or of the human condition for us; to remove that which is distorting its revelation to us. Further illustrations of this Renaissance understanding are found in Piero di Cosimo's *Hunting Scene* (circa 1495-1500) and *The Return from the Hunt* (circa 1495-1500).

*'Hunting Scene' by Piero di Cosimo, c. 1495-1500*
*(Metropolitan Museum of Art, New York)*

*'Return from the Hunt' by Piero di Cosimo, c. 1495-1500*
*(Metropolitan Museum of Art, New York)*

Through these works Piero sought to express the Epicurean account of existence, which had taken on a renewed interest owing to the discovery of the Latin philosophical poem *De Rerum Natura*. Confronting us with the brutality of primal existence, Piero seeks to express the Epicurean claim that the nonchalance of the gods to the human condition inspires our own freedom. Both Michaelangelo and Piero illustrate for us the Renaissance understanding that the representation of beauty through artistic expression is an exercise in representing an *actual world*. Concordant with that understanding, art was also to have a social purpose. As Suzi Gablik explains 'until we come to the modern epoch, all art had a social significance and a social obligation.'[60] Commissioned by the Renaissance religious and social elites, art was to be instructive as to the desirable human condition (the good) or the truth (whether religious or philosophical).

Forwarding to our own day, the movement from Renaissance art's search for true beauty and its wider social implications to postmodern art is ably illustrated by Marcel Duchamp's *Fountain*.

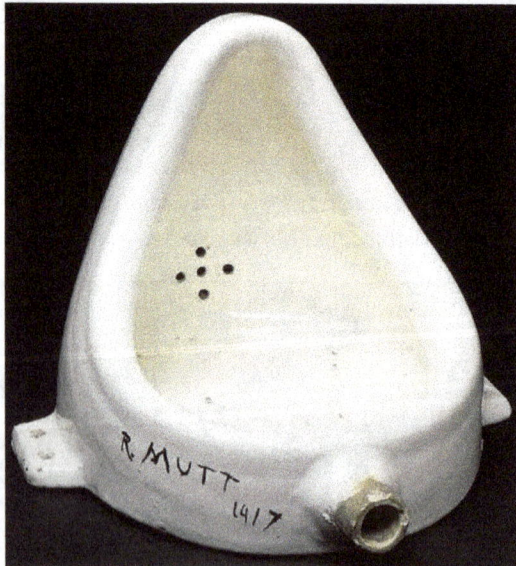

*'Fountain' by Marcel Duchamp, 1917*
*(Replica in Tate Gallery of Modern Art, London)*

---

[60] Suzi Gablik, *Has Modernism Failed?* (Thames and Hudson, 1984) 23.

In 1917 Duchamp's entrance of a signed mass-manufactured uri-
nal into a Society of Independent Artists exhibition to be held in
New York received both accolades and disdain. The intense response Duchamp inspired amongst his contemporaries signified
both the novelty and the profound consequence of his declaration.
*Fountain* was a cold, heartless statement of postmodern philosophy: there is no such thing as beauty in art, and thus there is no
such thing as her correlates, truth or the good. In repudiating the
aesthetic judgement and replacing it with the banal or ghastly, postmodern art expresses postmodernity's repudiation of beauty's classical relation with truth and with the good. However, as Scruton
has said, '[w]hat is shocking first time round is boring and vacuous
when repeated.'[61] Gablik similarly laments that in postmodern art
'notions of uninhibited individualist innovation ... have become a
sterile monotony.'[62] She writes that for the postmodern artist '[t]he
very idea of content was taken to be a hindrance and a nuisance,
and looking for meaning was a form of philistinism. The work is a
painted surface, nothing more, and its meaning is entirely an aesthetic one.'[63] Her concern is that, even where modern art retains a
role for beauty, it is cleaved of any relation to the true or the good.
This departure from Western art's historical concern for the common good has had dire consequence for our esteem of art: 'the artist's role has become marginal in modern Western society'.[64] This
modern eschewal of art's prior role in proclaiming truth and the
good is far from celebrated. The popular reaction against postmodern art is evidenced in the public ridicule of the price paid by the
Tate Gallery for *Equivalent VIII* by Carl Andre in 1972, and the
price paid for Jackson Pollock's *Blue Poles* by the National Gallery
of Australia in 1973. The former was popularly criticised as being

---

[61] British Broadcasting Corporation, *Why Beauty Matters* 06:45 (British Broadcasting Corporation, 2009).

[62] Gablik (n 60) 31.

[63] Ibid 22.

[64] Ibid 28.

nothing more than a 'pile of bricks' and the latter for being lines of paint randomly thrown on a canvass.

However, the collapse is not absolute and flickers of hope remain. Contemporary artists such as Michael Galovic preserve for us the relation of beauty to the good and the true, while deploying the tools of abstract art.[65]

'The Timeless Dance Triptych' by Michael Galovic, 2016

Galovic's *The Timeless Dance Triptych*,[66] commissioned for a girl's school in Essendon, adorns the cover of this book. In it Galovic celebrates the Biblical account of the rescue of the Israelites from slavery under the Egyptians. Comprised of three panels representing the past, the present and the future, the triptych gently suggests to the girls their own cause for celebration as the current protagonists in an age-old *agon*. The triptych presents the movement of the Israelites through time from slavery under the Egyptians, to the dance of Miriam after the escape from Egypt, to eternity. It emphasises the continuity between prior, current and future generations in our movement toward the eternal, 'the Christian idea of the incomplete leading contemplatively to the fulfilled.'[67] The first panel represents Israel's state prior to the Passover and

---

[65] Michael Galovic, *Sailing Back to Byzantium* (Yarra & Hunter Arts Press, 2024).

[66] *The Timeless Dance Triptych*, 2016, 120 x 120cm.

[67] Jina Mulligan, 'The Timeless Dance: A Sacred Work of Art by Michael Galovich', *Sailing Back to Byzantium* (Yarra & Hunter Arts Press, 2024) 232.

the journey out of slavery, echoing the Gospel account of our own state of slavery prior to the forgiveness offered through Christ. The central panel depicts the celebration and movement of Miriam's dance in light of that deliverance, representing the current temporal generation. The third panel represents the movement into the future and eternity. The three eras are bound together by subtle lines, emphasising their continuity. In her commentary on the work Mulligan writes '[e]ach work carries a hint of transcendent beauty and disappears momentarily into the divine. The process acts as an enabler to transcendence.'[68] Galovic is but one example of the vanguard continuing to assert art's role in proclaiming the true and the good to our society.[69]

This brief, illustrative survey of the movement from Renaissance to modern art demonstrates that contemporary art can be understood as a chronicle of the core dispute within modern aesthetics: is the object beautiful simply because we perceive beauty in it (the subjective argument), or is its beauty intrinsic and universal, regardless of any value we ascribe to it (the objective argument). The movement is also a chronicle of the emergence of the core claims of postmodernism: there is no beauty, there is no truth, there is no common good. Even when beauty is esteemed in modern art, it is of purely subjective interest, it has no relation to the truth or the good. Artists like Michael Galovic show us that the claims of postmodernism do not remain unchallenged. In these ways art mimics for us what many consider to be the core dispute of contemporary philosophy: is postmodernism to prevail against the classical triumvirate of beauty, the true and the good (whether according to the Jewish or Greek accounts)? In light of this survey perhaps GWF Hegel did then mine a vein of truth when he sought to discover

---

[68] Ibid 233.

[69] Of particular note see, eg, the other examples provided by Paul Hobbs, Paulo Medina, Maggy Masselter, Georges Rouault, James Tissot, and Judith Tutin.

an era's *Geist* within its art.[70] The law has been embroiled in this fight between competing philosophical codes, including, as I will now show, through the wielding of Hegel's insight to declare a new charitable purpose.

## The Law's Interface with Aesthetic Beauty

To draw this first lecture to a close I will now focus the themes developed thus far toward our specific investigation of beauty's interaction with the law. To do this I will first observe the encroachment of the subject/object problematic within our jurisprudence's attempts to define aesthetic beauty. I will then consider the recent outworking of Hegel's thesis of the *Geist* in Australian charity law, before concluding with a study in recent reforms declaring the relevance of beauty to architecture, environmental and planning law within the United Kingdom. These three encroachments of beauty within our jurisprudence have significant consequences for the contemporary debate as to whether postmodernism is to prevail against the beautiful, the true and the good. What we will see is, just as philosophy has subtly populated art, so philosophy imbues our jurisprudence.

To conduct the first of our three interrogations we must return to the dawn of the modern notion of the aesthetic, witnessed in Kant's *Critique of Judgement*. Therein Kant tackles the problematic fact that, although our regard for a beautiful object is inherently subjective, our judgement claims to be universally valid (as I have said, this being an assertion the nearby 'Grot' has testified to since 1668).[71]

---

[70] GWF Hegel, *Aesthetics: Lectures on Fine Art*, tr TM Knox (Clarendon, 1975). However, given this evidence of the continuing influence between art and philosophy within our postmodern age, perhaps Hegel was misguided in declaring the 'end of art' in the philosophy of the Enlightenment.

[71] Similarly, what David Hume called the 'aesthetic sense' was for him irreducible: 'ideas' (like the 'soul') are a 'production of something out of nothing', not 'even conceivable by the mind', 'beyond our comprehension'. David Hume, *An Enquiry Concerning Human Understanding* (Clarendon Press, 1902) 68; David Hume, *A Treatise of Human Nature* (Clarendon Press, 1896) 7; Manent, *The City of Man* (n 43) 144. Kant famously credited Hume with having awoken him

Kant tried to demonstrate that the implicit claim of the 'disinterested and *free* delight' of aesthetic judgement is valid for everyone.[72] The German word here translated as 'disinterest', *disinteresse*, in its contemporary context referred to a pleasure not grounded in the satisfaction of desire, including, for example, the desire to possess the object in question. As desire varies from person to person, to be universal, beauty must transcend the desire to possess. Alongside the many other Kantian notions given action by the French Revolution, his seminal understanding of the universality of the aesthetic sense found its expression in the French Revolutionaries' establishment of the first modern public art gallery in 1793, now the Louvre, on the then revolutionary understanding that aesthetic beauty could be accessed by all. Kant's idea that beauty could be universally valid (a Platonic notion) correlated with his core concept of the categorical imperative, holding that morality is universal and discernible to human reason without the need for divine revelation. Kant's belief in universal aesthetic sense and morality are not coherent with his insistence on the separation of the subjective world as we perceive it and the objective world as it is. Noting the intellectual continuum between Kant's separation of subject and object and postmodernism, and the dissonance of that continuum with Kant's belief in universal principles, Nietzsche surely expressed an acute insight when he described Kant as 'the great delayer'.[73]

In a campaign now ranging over multiple jurisprudential fronts, judges have waded into the *agon* raging over the fundamental questions of aesthetics: what is 'beauty' and what is 'art'? The Kantian assertion that a universally agreed notion of beauty is available to us through the pure aesthetic judgement has had profound implica-

---

from his 'dogmatic slumber'.

[72] Immanuel Kant, 'The Critique of Judgement' in Robert Maynard Hutchins (ed), *Great Books of the Western World: Kant* tr James Creed Meredith (Encyclopaedia Brittannica, 1952) 479, bk 1, ch 5 (emphasis in original). Malcolm Budd, 'Aesthetics', *Concise Routledge Encyclopedia of Philosophy* (Routledge, 2000) 9.

[73] George Grant, *English-Speaking Justice* (University of Notre Dame Press, 1985) 79. Thanks to Iain Benson for drawing this insightful quote to my attention.

tions within the common law of charitable trusts. That law recog-
nises that 'the education of the public taste may be a valid charitable
object'.[74] The same recognition is accorded to a 'purpose of raising
the artistic taste and musical appreciation of the citizens of ... the
public'.[75] The Kantian and French Revolutionary belief in the universality of aesthetic taste is plainly exhibited in South Australian
Supreme Court Justice Sir Herbert Mayo's assertion that 'the development of the aesthetic sense in the appreciation of ... beautiful and
attractive objects whether they be pictures, statuary, or other things
that may allure delight or intrigue the senses' is for the public benefit, and hence charitable.[76] The Kantian hope is also expressed in
Master of the Rolls Lord Greene's assertion that '[t]he education
of artistic taste is one of the most important things in the development of a civilised human being'.[77] It is redolent within Justice
Vaisey's affirmation that a gift to bring the 'masterpieces of fine art
within the reach of the people of Ireland of all classes' is for the
public benefit.[78]

This common law doctrine has led judges to the unfortunate position of policing Kant's philosophical boundary between the beautiful appreciable to our disinterested pleasure, and the banal or plain
ugly. In the famous *Re Pinion (deceased)* ('*Pinion's case*') a gift of a
studio, paintings and furniture as a collection to form an exhibition
was described by Lord Justice Harman as follows:

> there is a strong body of evidence here that as a means
> of education this collection is worthless. The testator's
> own paintings, of which there are over fifty, are said by
> competent persons to be in an academic style and 'atro-
> ciously bad' and the other pictures without exception to

[74] *Commissioners of Inland Revenue v White* (1980) 55 TC 651, 655 (Fox J).

[75] *Re Perpetual Trustees Queensland Ltd* [2000] 2 Qd R 647, 658 [39] (Williams J).

[76] *Re Chanter (deceased)* [1952] SASR 299, 302 (Mayo J).

[77] *Royal Choral Society v Commissioners of Inland Revenue* [1943] 2 All ER 101,
104-5 (Lord Greene MR).

[78] *Re Shaw's Will Trusts* [1952] 1 Ch 163, 171-2 (Vaisey J).

be worthless ... Indeed one of the experts expresses his surprise that so voracious a collector should not by hazard have picked up even one meritorious object ... I can conceive of no useful object to be served in foisting on the public this mass of junk. It has neither public utility nor educative value.[79]

These judgements evidence the law's acceptance of Kant's belief in the universality of the aesthetic judgment. The law is thus cast as a protagonist in the debate surrounding the subject/object conundrum. In accepting that there is such a thing as objective beauty it comes down on the side of unity between object and subject. Whether consciously or not, the law thus stakes a claim in the contemporary debates concerning truth and the good inspired by the emergence of postmodernism. In this the law declares its hand against Nietzsche's desire to 'thrash him' who asserts 'the true', 'the good and the beautiful are one'.[80]

The common law of charities goes even further when, imbibing the groundbreaking thesis of Hegel, it accepts the claim that art may instantiate a culture's own philosophical distinctiveness in a manner not immediately perceptible to its own inhabitants.[81] In that recognition the law admits the classical claim of a relation between beauty and truth. Consider, for example, the 2001 Australian *Charities Definition Inquiry's* description of the charitable purpose of 'advancing culture':

> Like language, the arts are one of the principal means by which a society binds itself together and transmits its beliefs and standards from one generation to another. The arts perform this function when they embody, reinforce and celebrate the values of their society, when they confirm and exemplify the lessons simultaneously taught

---

[79]   *Re Pinion (deceased)* [1964] 1 All ER 890, 894 (Harman LJ).

[80]   Nietzsche, *The Will to Power* (n 58) 465, §822.

[81]   Hegel (n 70).

by the family, by the formal structures of education, and by the mass media in all their variety. In this function the arts play a critically important role. Not only do they provide a kind of social 'glue', but they also furnish a means by which society can identify and distinguish itself from others.[82]

As authority for this proposition the Inquiry quoted the Australian novelist, short story writer, poet and playwright David Malouf:

The uniqueness of a people can be invisible to those who know it only as an everyday thing. We do not always see, from within, the extent to which the things that we make are intimate reflections of us, of a local way of doing things, of thinking and feeling and interpreting. We delight in the energy these things give us, the sense we get of being alive and in our own skins. What we do not see is that the energy itself is of a unique kind, that there is a peculiar freshness and originality in the way we take what is classic and remake it as our own. It is here, unconsciously perhaps, that we catch the clearest image of ourselves as Australians; and this confirmation of identity too we take back into our lives and use in all sorts of productive and imaginative ways. What outsiders recognise as original and unique, we experience simply as what we are, what we have discovered by reflection from what we have made, and which nothing else could have revealed to us.[83]

Solzhenitsyn asserted a similar conclusion in his Nobel Prize in Literature acceptance lecture: 'In this way [art, specifically litera-

---

[82] I Sheppard, R Fitzgerald and D Gonski (Commonwealth of Australia), *Report of the Inquiry into the Definition of Charities and Related Organisations*, 28 June 2001) 182 citing Simone Weil, *A Cabinet of Curiosities: Inquiries into Museums and their Prospects* (Smithsonian Institute Press, 1995).

[83] David Malouf, 'Foreword', *Securing our Future: Major Performing Arts Inquiry* (Discussion Paper, July 1999) quoted in Sheppard, Fitzgerald and Gonski (n 82) 182.

ture] becomes the living memory of nations. In this way it cherishes and nourishes within itself the nation's lost history in a form not
susceptible to distortion and slander. And thereby, together with
language, it preserves the national soul.'[84] Solzhenitsyn's belief in
beauty as a society's ultimate preserve of truth bears all the more
weight when it is recalled that it comes to us from a man writing
from within the Soviet State, in which he was effectively impris-
oned. His claim was not without evidential basis. From within the
confines of that State he attested to the preservative and redemptive
effects of Tolstoy's and Dostoyevsky's writings, who, owing to their
momentous contribution to the Russian cultural *Geist*, the Soviets
dared not ban. In essence Gablik's critique of postmodern art is that
it has eschewed its role in preserving 'the national soul'. To illustrate
this claim, she contrasts modern art with medieval art, wherein 'the
artist exalted the dominant values of his society, and society in turn
recognized itself in an art that was expressive of its values.'[85] To
the extent the charitable purpose of 'advancing culture' relies on
this social role of art (according to the reasoning of the *Charities
Definition Inquiry*), Gablik's critique would call into question the
charitable status of museums of contemporary art. They would be
left relying only on the aesthetic value of the works they exhibit.

In making a distinction between objects of aesthetic value and
those without, the law makes a claim as to the objective nature of
beauty. Similarly, in making a distinction between those artifacts
that embody the *Geist* of a people and those that do not, the law
makes a claim as to the interaction between beauty and truth. When
seen against the backdrop of the contemporary contest between
the classical relation of beauty, the true and the good and the postmodern eschewal of that relation, in charity law our jurisprudence
declares upon the side of beauty, truth and the good. It does so in
defiance of the Enlightenment separation of object and subject and
its culmination in postmodernism's denial of any common denomi-

---

[84] Solzhenitsyn (n 1) 18.
[85] Gablik (n 60) 29.

nator. Under the influence of these deep philosophical currents, whether consciously or not, our law finds itself a protagonist in the debates inspired by the emergence of postmodernism.

Recent amendments to architecture, planning and environmental jurisprudence in the United Kingdom provide further evidence of the law's defiance. Scruton claims that for architecture, context is everything: 'True architects do not subdue their material to some external purpose; they *converse* with it, allowing the material to interrogate the space in which they build.'[86] Defying Le Corbusier's modernist dictum that 'a house is a machine for living in'[87] Scruton asserts that the search for a home is the search for place encountered as a subject, not just an object; 'to find inscribed in the world of objects some record of our personal concerns.'[88] He connects this search to beauty when he asserts 'the love of beauty is founded in the need for settlement, for a place that we share, where, as Hölderlin puts it ... "all seems familiar, even the casual greeting seems like a friend's and every face belongs".'[89] You will be familiar with the power of context if you have ever witnessed a beautiful street besmirched by a new structure in a discordant style (even where that new structure, viewed in isolation, has its own beautiful features).

These principles have recently made their way into UK planning law, consequent on the recommendations of the *Building Better, Building Beautiful Commission* review co-chaired by Scruton. Declaring that 'ugly' 'buildings violate the context in which they are placed ... destroy the sense of place, undermine the spirit of community, and ensure that we are not at home in our world', the Review concluded:

> beauty ... includes everything that promotes a healthy

---

[86] Scruton (n 50) 128 (emphasis in original).
[87] Charles-Édouard Jeanneret aka Le Corbusier quoted in ibid 130.
[88] Ibid 130-1.
[89] Friedrich Hölderlin *Heimkunft* quoted in ibid 135.

and happy life, everything that makes a collection of buildings into a place, everything that turns anywhere into somewhere, and nowhere into home. So understood beauty should be an essential condition for the grant of planning permission.[90]

Here the Commission expressly asserts the relation between beauty and the good life. Following upon these recommendations the *National Planning Policy Framework* is now replete with references to 'beauty'. The Framework is structured around three broad limbs, one of which is the 'social objective', given expression 'by fostering well-designed, *beautiful* and safe places'.[91] The Framework states that '[s]trategic policies should ... ensure outcomes support *beauty* and placemaking)';[92] that '[p]lanning policies and decisions should contribute to and enhance the natural and local environment by: ... recognising the intrinsic character and *beauty* of the countryside';[93] 'that appropriate tools such as masterplans and design guides or codes are used to secure a variety of well-designed and *beautiful* homes';[94] that '[p]lanning policies and decisions should aim to achieve healthy, inclusive and safe places and *beautiful* buildings'[95] and take into regard the 'importance of securing well-designed and *beautiful*, attractive and healthy places';[96] and that '[t]he creation of high quality, *beautiful* and sustainable buildings and places is fundamental to what the planning and development process should

---

[90] Building Better Building Beautiful Commission, 'Living with Beauty: Promoting Health, Well-Being and Sustainable Growth' (Report, January 2020) iv <https://assets.publishing.service.gov.uk/media/5e3191a9ed915d0938933263/Living_with_beauty_BBBBC_report.pdf>.

[91] Ministry of Housing Communities and Local Government, 'National Planning Policy Framework', (December 2023) [8(b)] (emphasis added) <https://assets.publishing.service.gov.uk/media/669a25e9a3c2a28abb50d2b4/NPPF_December_2023.pdf>.

[92] Ibid [20] (emphasis added).

[93] Ibid [180(b)] (emphasis added).

[94] Ibid [74(c)] (emphasis added).

[95] Ibid [96] (emphasis added).

[96] Ibid [128(e)] (emphasis added).

achieve.[97] Again we encounter a legal endorsement of the existence
of an objective world of beauty. However, the new regime has thrust
upon decision makers the difficult task of distinguishing the beautiful from the ugly. In a recent planning appeal the Delegate of the
Secretary of State posited the following indicia for discerning archi-
tectural 'beauty':

> the research presented as … evidence demonstrates that
> the most attractive places in London were best predicated
> by the following: distance to a listed building, high built-
> up area and density, richness of land uses and urban fur-
> niture, the immediate presence of a listed building, rich-
> ness of commercial activities, a high average proportion
> of pre-1939 buildings and generous proportions between
> footways and carriageways.

Decision Officer Stasiak also made clear that 'local context' is relevant in the determination of what is architecturally 'beautiful'.[98]
Again the law declares on the side of a real world of beauty in the
contemporary debate inspired by Nietzsche's instruction to 'thrash
him' who asserts 'the true', 'the good and the beautiful are one'.[99] Indeed for the law beauty is sufficiently universal and 'real' as to enable
the evidencing of its presence in a given locality.

## Beauty in Relation to Justice

We have commenced our journey into beauty and the law by trac-
ing through intellectual history and art the development of postmodernism and its consequences for the classical relation between
beauty, the true and the good. That interrogation has positioned

---

[97] Ibid [131] (emphasis added).

[98] Department for Levelling Up Housing & Communities, 'Decision on Correction Notice under Section 57 of the Planning and Compulsory Purchase Act
2004, Application made by MEC London Property 3 (General Partner) Limited
regarding former London Television Centre, 60-72 Upper Ground, London,
SE1 9LT' (Application Ref: 21/02668/EIAFUL, (Decision Officer Stasiak), 09
February 2024).

[99] Nietzsche, *The Will to Power* (n 58) 465, §822.

us to ask: if we reject the notion of beauty, what is to hold back the rejection of truth or the good? The rejection of any one of the three transcendentals leads to the rejection of any of the others, as postmodern art so defiantly declares for us. But what then, the lawyer must ask, is to hold back the rejection of justice? CS Lewis succinctly draws out the consequences of modernity's rending asunder the subject and the object for justice: 'The world of facts, without trace of value, and the world of feelings, without one trace of truth or falsehood, justice or injustice, confront one another, and no *rapprochement* is possible.'[100] In the next lecture I will argue that the claims of justice highlight the momentous significance of the incoherence lying at the heart of postmodernism. As John Lennox has said, postmodernism proceeds from 'a patent self-contradiction. It expects us to accept, as absolute truth, that there are no absolute truths.'[101]

This inescapable incoherence is one which has great salience for the proper administration of justice. For the lawyer whose practice encounters injustice postmodernism presents a distinct affront. Iain Benson identifies the irony of the postmodernist's claim for justice: 'They will rail against injustice having denied that there can be objective goods.'[102] However, as CS Lewis has asserted: 'It is no use trying to "see through" first principles. If you see through everything, then everything is transparent. But a wholly transparent world is an invisible world. To "see through" all things is the same as not to see.'[103] When justice is depicted as blindfolded, she is blind to personal bias. She is not blind to the *real occurrence of injustice*, or the *actual moral value* of the just outcome. In the next lecture I will build upon our encounter with the pre-Enlightenment Jewish and Greek accounts of the relationship between beau-

---

[100]  Lewis, *The Abolition of Man* (n 45) 13.

[101]  John C Lennox, *Against the Flow* (Monarch Books, 2015) 39.

[102]  Iain T Benson, 'The Relationship Between Beauty and Justice' (Lecture, Roundtable for the Western Heritage Association, 21 February 2023) 11.

[103]  Lewis, *The Abolition of Man* (n 45) 50.

ty, truth and the good to explore the relation of beauty to injustice. In so doing we will seek to locate upon the profound and ongoing reply the law has to offer against the postmodern account.

## Lecture 1 Group Discussion Questions

1. In what ways, if any, has your professional life led to an engagement with 'beauty'?

2. Recount a time when you found something profoundly beautiful or in which you engaged with the sublime. Did this inform your relationship with God in any way?

3. Do you see these experiences as having any implications for your sense of vocation?

4. How might your working life be changed by a renewed understanding of the role of beauty in our lives?

# LECTURE 2

## *Beauty and Injustice*

In the previous lecture we saw that, by deploying Kant's understanding of aesthetic appreciation as 'disinterested' subjective feelings of pleasure in perceptual appearance, the law had found itself in the invidious position of policing the philosophical boundary between the banal and the beautiful. However, while Kant accepted that beauty could be universal, he ultimately laid the seeds for postmodernism by denying human access to objective reality by any means whatsoever. This denial was found in his distinction between the subjective world we perceive and conceive and the objective world in itself; ultimate noumenal reality independent of the subjective viewer, and for Kant, unknowable. It was argued that postmodernism's consequent eschewal of the belief in objective beauty closely parallels its denial of an ascription to objective truth and the notion of a common good. However, in charity and planning law we found multiple declarations against the claims of postmodernism and on the side of objective beauty and its relationship with the true and the good. Noting the close association of both truth and the good with justice, this second lecture will put these arguments to further work in formulating a theoretical framework, a *causa agendi*, sufficient to sustain just action for those who seek to direct their professional labours to the common good.

## Postmodernism's Influence Upon Popular Culture

Postmodernism wields significant influence upon contemporary Western culture. Its emergence as a philosophical powerhouse has laid the foundations for a world riven by paradox. In the dim afterglow of Enlightenment reasoning we still hear echoes of the claim that human nature is basically good and, with Hegelian optimism, that through the exercise of reason society will proceed to an ever greater end. Yet the horrors of the twentieth century offer a significant challenge to this aspiration. Postmodernism takes the Kantian refusal to admit we can know objective reality and boldly asserts that there is no truth. Paradoxically, existentialism tells us your authentic self is inescapable, and that the goal of life is the perpetual expression of that authentic self; that ultimately the only truth that matters is your own individual subjective reality.

If the incoherence within contemporary societal tropes can teach us anything it is that, if politics is downstream of culture, culture is downstream of philosophy. Popular culture is imbued with philosophy precisely because philosophy concerns itself with matters that are fascinating to the human mind. For these reasons popular culture is today suffuse with the claims of postmodernism. When Kelly Clarkson sings 'what doesn't kill you makes you stronger' she directly announces Nietzschean philosophy to my unsuspecting twelve year old daughter.[104] Nietzsche's central claim that existence will never be the same for 'God is dead … And we have killed him!'[105] is being deposited into her subconscious when Harry Styles sings on repeat:

> In this world, it's just us
> You know it's not the same as it was
> In this world, it's just us
> You know it's not the same as it was
> As it was, as it was
> You know it's not the same …

His lyrics embody contemporary existentialist anguish. Styles, whether he is aware of it or not, is reaping the rewards of postmodernism's denial of beauty, truth and the good, for his song goes on:

> Answer the phone
> "Harry, you're no good alone

---

[104] Friedrich Nietzsche, *Twilight of the Idols and The Anti-Christ*, tr RJ Hollingdale (Penguin, 2003) 33.

[105] Friedrich Nietzsche, *The Gay Science*, tr Josefine Nauckhoff and Adrian Del Caro (Cambridge University Press, 2001) 120, $126.

Why are you sitting at home on the floor?

What kind of pills are you on?"

Ringin' the bell

And nobody's coming to help ...

Styles presents us with a study in the contemporary consequences of effecting Nietzsche's claims that 'God is dead' and that anyone who ascribes to beauty, truth or the good should be 'thrash[ed]',[106] presented on a silver platter for consumption by twelve year old boys and girls the world over. However, while Styles grapples with his isolation, Miley Cyrus boldly asserts liberalism's founding notion of the wholeness of the isolated individual when she tells us that

I can buy myself flowers

Write my name in the sand

Talk to myself for hours

Say things you don't understand

I can take myself dancing

And I can hold my own hand

Yeah, I can love me better than you can ...

These paragons of modern culture disclose no apparent self-awareness as to how they are contributing to, indeed modelling for us, the malaise of despondency instigated by contemporary Western culture.

The Canadian philosopher Charles Taylor challenges us to see how the culmination of our intellectual history in postmodernism has birthed 'the reality of alienation in our societies.'[107] Oliver O'Donovan argues that this contagion of alienation is the inevitable consequence of giving reign to a political philosophy founded squarely upon individual autonomy. He asserts that the founding liberal theory of individual autonomy binds the citizen in a state of permanent potentiality:

Perpetually oriented to the elusive moment of imme-

---

[106] Nietzsche, *The Will to Power* (n 58) 465, §822.

[107] Charles Taylor, *A Secular Age* (Harvard University Press, 2007) 411.

diacy, the modern subject stands aloof from his own kind, reflecting objectively upon it, subordinating it to the logic of affective detachment, holding back from participation ... The subject thus in course of constant self-construction is 'unsituated.' ... it is defined by its consciousness. It has no face.[108]

Oliver O'Donovan and John Milbank seek to model their analysis of liberalism's founding tenets on Augustine's deconstruction of the mythology of Roman political philosophy in *The City of God*. Augustine argued that the actual 'god' worshipped by the Romans was that of 'the injustice of foreigners'.[109] The need for a theoretical justification for the continual extension of Empire was the real source fuelling the perpetual worship of this 'god'. The Romans were justified in making unending war by the barbarity of those they conquered. For this reason Scipio 'refused to agree to the destruction of Carthage', recognising that the necessity of violence against an external enemy was the preserve of Rome's unity.[110] John Milbank thus argues that the continual expansion of Empire was necessary for Rome to perpetuate its founding myths: 'a "preceding" anarchy and arbitrary domination must always be newly sought out if the founding story is again to be re-enacted'.[111]

Deploying O'Donovan's critique of liberal autonomy we might apply a similar analysis to the founding tenets of liberalism: the 'elusive moment of immediacy' in which the modern subject is engaged in a 'constant' exercise of 'self-construction' necessitates a perpetual cycle of disavowing whatever 'face' it might momentarily have displayed. O'Donovan's picture of the liberal individual enslaved to the perpetual moment of reinvention at the altar of her own autonomy explicates the modern tension at the heart of liberal-conservative political partnerships. Gablik applies this

---

[108] Oliver O'Donovan, *The Ways of Judgement* (William B Eerdmans, 2005) 310.
[109] Augustine (n 12) 196 bk 4, ch 15.
[110] Ibid 147, bk 1, ch 30. See also 159-60, bk 2, ch 18.
[111] Milbank (n 42) 394.

cycle to aesthetics when she argues that '[i]ndividualism and antitraditionalism are one and the same psychological force' at work in contemporary art.[112]

TS Eliot offers an exquisitely phrased critique of this liberal penchant for perpetual reinvention in *East Coker*. Eliot asserts that our 'home' cannot be created or sustained by a perpetual stream of inchoate, unrelated instinctual urges. Instead 'home' is comprised of the relation between the accruing lifetime of one's experiences and the undecipherable influence of one's forebears:

> Not the intense moment
> Isolated, with no before and after,
> But a lifetime burning in every moment
> And not the lifetime of one man only
> But of old stones that cannot be deciphered.[113]

For Eliot, the conservative cherishes as a gift of beauty that which her preceding generations, with the benefit of their experience, savoured as estimable. Contrary to the conservative inclination, the dynamic of autonomy has fuelled the postmodern claim that the old moral codes of Athens and Jerusalem no longer have value for us. Nietzsche's Zaruthustra stands for the proposition that, in the words of CS Lewis: '"Good" and "bad" applied to [post-modern man], are words without content: for it is from [post-modern man] that the content of these words is henceforward to be derived.'[114]

As Harry Styles shows, this individualising and secularising revolution has had marked and deleterious effects on mental and physical health, now prompting a range of Governmental responses.[115] In 2018 Theresa May reflected the increasing awareness of

---

[112] Gablik (n 60) 30.

[113] Eliot, 'East Coker' (n 5) 28.

[114] Lewis, *The Abolition of Man* (n 45) 40. See Friedrich Nietzsche, *Thus Spoke Zarathustra*, tr RJ Hollingdale (Penguin Books, 1961).

[115] John Cacioppo and William Patrick, *Loneliness* (WW Norton, 2008); Jo Abbott et al, 'The Impact of Loneliness on the Health and Wellbeing of Australians' (2018) 40(6) *InPsych*.

the prevalence of 'isolation' and its effects when she announced England's first Minister for Loneliness.[116] At the time of writing, the New South Wales Parliament has convened an Inquiry into the 'prevalence, causes and impacts of loneliness'.[117] Phillip Blond writes that '[m]any are sceptical that these trends can be reversed, seeing anomic individualism and norm-less social interactions as inevitable conditions of modernity.'[118] Given the rise of postmodernism, the challenge for liberalism remains: to defy these allegations by affording the space for beauty, truth and the good to make their continuing claims upon us.

## The Hope of Justice

Notwithstanding the bleak picture painted by these critics of liberalism and postmodernism, there remains many reasons for hope. One source of optimism comes to us from a most unexpected place: the criminal law. Almost every evening the nightly news presents a potent riposte to the claims of postmodernism. On the steps of the courthouse following the delivery of judgement the families of the victims customarily say one of two things: 'justice was served here today', or 'justice was denied here today'. Their personal encounter with injustice presents a direct retort to postmodernism's claim that there is no truth, no good and no beauty. In a recent lecture given under the title 'The Relation Between Beauty and Justice' Iain Benson summarised the deep communication between these two concepts:

> the opposite of beauty is injury the second syllable of
> which word is the same root as the word for justice and
> this concept of justice - rendering to God or to others

---

[116] Prime Minister's Office, 'PM Launches Government's First Loneliness Strategy', *gov.uk* (Press Release, 16 October 2018) <https://www.gov.uk/government/news/pm-launches-governments-first-loneliness-strategy>; Department for Digital Culture Media and Sport, *A Connected Society*, (October 2018).

[117] New South Wales Parliament Standing Committee on Social Issues, 'Prevalence, Causes and Impacts of Loneliness in New South Wales', *parliament.nsw. gov.au* (Web Page, 06 August 2024) <https://www.parliament.nsw.gov.au/committees/inquiries/Pages/inquiry-details.aspx?pk=3066>.

[118] Phillip Blond, *Red Tory* (Faber and Faber, 2010) 81.

what is their due, reminds us that justice and beauty share the term "fair". In the arts, "fairness" means beauty of countenance and in law "justice as fairness" has to do [with], as John Rawls noted a certain "symmetry of our relations with one another."[119]

Permit me to explore this communication through a personal illustration. The weightiest encounter I have had with the reality of injustice in this world was on a joint trip between the Lawyers' Christian Fellowship and the Australian Christian Legal Society to Rwanda in 2011. I can still see the faces of the countless children looking back at me from the photos that covered the walls in the genocide museum in Kigali. My initial response when seeing their beautiful innocent faces was immense pain and sadness at the pure injustice of their deaths. However, as the rooms of pictures rolled on, and as the faces kept presenting themselves to me, the realisation that each child was a world in their own, was a world in their own to their own parents, to their family and friends, gave rise to a horrifying sense of dread. Suddenly my gaze upon these photos became horrendous because it could not contain the meaning of that which I looked upon; my gaze became an affront to their meaning. And yet they must be recalled. The pointless, inexplicable cruelty was debilitating.

The most horrifying realisation is that this cruelty did not occur in a remote concentration camp but instead through one-on-one encounters in villages all across the country. The Rwandan genocide saw villagers inexplicably take up machetes to butcher their lifetime neighbours. The genocide memorial was the most potent reply to the Enlightenment claim that human nature is basically good that I have ever encountered. Like the families on the nightly news in our own countries, the cry for justice of the families of those small Rwandan children living on in the remembrance inspired by the genocide memorial makes postmodernism's claim that there is no

---

[119] Benson (n 102) 9.

truth, no beauty, and no good a cruel, depraved and monstrous distortion. Plainly stated, if there is no objective truth or reality, what possible account can we provide for seeking justice for the victim? In these ways the cry for justice defies the postmodern account.

And yet, it is widely accepted that the horrors of the twentieth century, and in particular World Wars One and Two, propelled postmodernism's wider acceptance within popular culture. It seems that the pointless loss of life on the battlefields of France, in the Pacific, in the concentration camps and in the gulags of Russia, could offer no other confirmation than to prove Nietzsche's radical claim that 'God is dead'.[120] This movement was nowhere better summarised than in TS Eliot's writings in the 1920s, penned before his conversion to Christianity. *The Love Song of J Alfred Prufrock* is his first celebrated study into modernity's abandonment of meaning. It commences with the following invitation:

> Let us go then, you and I,
> Where the evening is spread out against the sky
> Like a patient etherised upon a table ...[121]

In modernity even nature is propelled into a despondent state of oblivion. The subsequent portrait of modern existence Eliot presents in *The Wasteland* is one suffused with futility, evoking the pointless tragedy visited on Europe less than a decade before:

> Unreal City,
> Under the brown fog of a winter dawn,
> A crowd flowed over London Bridge, so many,
> I had not thought death had undone so many.
> Sighs, short and infrequent, were exhaled,
> And each man fixed his eyes before his feet.[122]

The long shadow of the war continues to reach us today. It is

---

[120] Nietzsche, *The Gay Science* (n 105) 120, §126.

[121] TS Eliot, 'The Love Song of J Alfred Prufrock', *Selected Poems* (Faber and Faber, 1954) 3.

[122] TS Eliot, 'The Waste Land' in Margaret Ferguson, Mary Jo Salter and Jon Stallworthy (eds), *The Norton Anthology of Poetry* (WW Norton, 5th ed, 2005) 1346.

no doubt a good thing that I, as a sixteen year old schoolboy, was required to read Erich Maria Remarque's *All Quiet on the Western Front* and that it remains on the curriculum today. The book had personal relevance, providing me with a greater understanding of, and reverence for, my great-grandfather's service on the Western Front, and the bravery of his younger brother who lost his life there. Having read it, I never did look again with the same eyes on the fading photo of those two innocent young men standing alongside my proud great-great-grandmother in their Black Watch kilts before their deployment to France. I also recall the deep outrage against the injustice and futility of the conflict that Remarque's work prompted in me. I was left with the haunting realisation that that could have been me had I been born of that time, or it yet still could be me, if war were to break out in our own time. Our natural personal outrage against such injustice, and the possibility of its recurrence, rightly defies the claim that there is no truth.

Yet, as noted in my opening remarks yesterday, it was against the horrors and injustice of the twenty-first century that Solzhenitsyn audaciously affirmed the irrepressible relevance of beauty in its relation to truth and the good: '[y]ou look into it and you glimpse – not yourself: you glimpse for an instant the Inaccessible, whither you can never gallop or fly. And only a deep yearning remains.'[123] Elaine Scarry has written:

> a special problem arises for beauty once the realm of the sacred is no longer believed or aspired to. If a beautiful young girl … or a small bird, or a glass vase, or a poem, or a tree has the metaphysical in behind it, that realm verifies the weight and attention we confer on the girl, bird, vase, poem, tree. But if the metaphysical realm has vanished, one may feel bereft not only because of the giant deficit left by that vacant realm but because the girl, the bird, the vase, the book now seem unable in their solitude to justify or account for the weight of their own

---

[123] Solzhenitsyn (n 1) 13.

beauty. If each calls out for attention that has no destination beyond itself, each seems self-centred, too fragile to support the gravity of our immense regard.[124]

Can the weight and attention I placed on those photos of the beautiful Rwandan children lost to the genocide be sustained if those children have indeed no metaphysical value? Surely, we cannot find any postmodern author that would tell us this, but if truth is now all relative, which tells us that there is no truth, on what basis do we mark their loss? Rwanda sets before us the evidence that something is deeply amiss with postmodernism. In this haunting way, the photos of the Rwandan children at the genocide memorial illustrate for us the depth of the dialogue between beauty and justice.

For Solzhenitsyn the barbarity of the twentieth century provoked not postmodernism's acceptance, but its antithesis. Rather than driving Solzhenitsyn toward postmodernism, as the surfeit of injustice within the twentieth century has done for popular culture, the brutality propelled him to defiantly reaffirm the ongoing role of the truth and of the good as expressed through beauty. Defying despondency, Solzhenitsyn asserts in his 1970 Nobel Prize in Literature acceptance speech that art shows us that

> that old trinity of Truth, Goodness and Beauty is not simply an empty shopworn formula after all ... For if the tops of these three trees converge, as the sages said they did, and the obvious and too straight growths of Truth and Goodness have been stifled, cut back and not allowed to flourish, then perhaps the fantastical, unpredictable and astonishing growths of beauty will break through and soar up *to the same place* and there do the work of all three?[125]

Recall that Solzhenitsyn expressed his hope in the role of art and beauty to connect us to eternal truth, to the good and to justice from within the Soviet Union, which did not welcome the making of

---

[124] Elaine Scarry, *On Beauty and Being Just* (Princeton University Press, 1999) 47.
[125] Solzhenitsyn (n 1) 13 (emphasis in original).

the award and from which he could not depart to accept it for fear of not being able to return. For Solzhenitsyn, a victim of the profound injustice of the gulags, his belief in the role of beauty was no ethereal matter. As I noted in the prior lecture, his hope that beauty would prevail to ultimately preserve truth, justice and goodness expressed his estimation of the role of writers such as Dostoyevsky and Tolstoy as repositories of truth in the Soviet era. For Solzhenitsyn the role of art in preserving justice was no forlorn hope. He wrote: 'But works that have drawn upon the truth and present us with it in vivid concentrated form take hold of us and grapple us to them masterfully, and no-one afterwards, not even centuries later, can refute those works.'[126] With this account of the role of art in hand, in this second lecture we will interrogate the relation of beauty to injustice with the aim of charting a theoretical framework sufficient to enable just action toward the common good.

## Theodicy and the Problem of Evil

Let's start in the shallows with theodicy and problem of evil. A theodicy is 'a justifying explanation of why God permits evil, responding to the problem of evil.'[127] Rwanda demands such an explanation. So do the countless lost to the wars of the past century. Augustine sought a theodicy in the fourth century when he set out to answer the questions: 'Where is evil then, and whence, and how it crept in hither? What is its root, and what its seed?'[128] How is it, he asked, that 'I should be gratuitously evil, having no temptation to ill but the ill itself'?[129] The Rwandan genocide presents the very same question: how could any person be provoked to such violence against his neighbour? The question of evil is of immense relevance for the lawyer who daily deals with evil's consequence, injustice.

From our earliest age we protest against injustice. Those of you

---

[126] Ibid.

[127] Ted Honderich (ed), *Oxford Companion to Philosophy* (Oxford University Press, 1995) 870.

[128] Augustine, 'The Confessions' (n 12) 45, bk 7, ch 5.

[129] Ibid 11, bk 2, ch 4.

with young children know just how long your willingness to lovingly demonstrate the authoritative power of tempered Enlightenment reason can hold out against the repeated remonstrance 'that's not fair Dad!' It's amazing how quickly the glib, 'Yeah well sometimes life's just like that kid' can emerge (surely there's yet a case to be made for the benefits of tempering juvenile expectations of justice with a little early dose of the Nietzschean *amor fati* (the love of fate)?) The theodicy offered within the Biblical account is clear that not all will be right in this present world. The book of Daniel is clear; martyrs will die prior to the return of the Messiah.[130] Just in case we were left in any doubt, the last book of the Bible again affirms it for us.[131] There is comfort in these prophecies alone: they tell us that our suffering is not without God's knowledge. As Andrew Myers has said in his contribution to the Lawyers' Christian Fellowship's compilation of daily devotionals for lawyers *Faithful and Fruitful:* 'When we understand that even God's children will experience suffering in this age, it relieves us of the stress and burdens of false expectations, freeing us up to glorify God and persevere in hardship.'[132] God's foreknowledge of our suffering declares that it remains subject to His absolute ultimate authority, His providence and power. Accordingly, the book of Revelation confirms the Bible's final word on the matter of suffering: '"He will wipe every tear from their eyes. There will be no more death" or mourning or crying or pain, for the old order of things has passed away.'[133]

Although the Bible assures us that suffering will occur, it is unwavering in its claim that God too shares our cry against the injustices of this temporal world. We are given countless occasions in which God protests against injustice. In answering the suffering Job from 'out of the whirlwind' God asks:

---

[130] Daniel 7:21. See Lennox (n 101) ch 16.

[131] Revelation 13:7.

[132] Andrew Myers, '03 January Looking Forward to the Year Ahead', *Faithful and Fruitful: 365 Daily Devotions Written by Lawyers for Lawyers* (The Lawyers' Christian Fellowship, 2023) 8.

[133] Revelation 21:4.

Have you ever given orders to the morning,
or shown the dawn its place,
that it might take the earth by the edges
and shake the wicked out of it?[134]

The implication is clear: God desires that 'the dawn … might take the earth by the edges and shake the wicked out of it'. In Isaiah we are told that God himself is 'appalled' that there was no one to intervene against injustice. He is so appalled that He Himself is moved to respond:

Truth is nowhere to be found, and whoever shuns evil becomes a prey. The LORD looked and was displeased that there was no justice. He saw that there was no one, he was appalled that there was no one to intervene; so his own arm achieved salvation for him, and his own righteousness sustained him.[135]

Permit me to illustrate the Bible's account of the relation of beauty and injustice with another personal illustration. Some years ago, I was invited to a developing country (which will remain unnamed) with a view to assisting in the establishment of a legal aid office, on the model of the existing CLEAR legal aid offices in Africa.[136] The country was then experimenting with a new level of civil society freedoms. Although there was a clear sense of expectation within the country, there remained much trepidation that the tentative reforms would not last. I entered a pre-arranged meeting with Civil Society Ministry Heads to be greeted by a man in full military regalia seated alone on an ornate wooden embossed couch, accompanied on his left by a line of five similarly dressed men in uniforms of differing colours seated along the wall. The General sitting on the

---

[134] Job 38:12-13.
[135] Isaiah 59:15-16.
[136] CLEAR (Christian Legal Education Aid and Research) is the mission arm of the Australian Christian Legal Society and the Lawyer's Christian Fellowship in the United Kingdom. For further information, see clear.org.au and https://lawcf.org/international/give-to-clear.

couch introduced his Department heads, all of whom shouted what I presumed to be 'yes sir!' in the local language as he announced them down the line.

The first words the General-cum-'Civil Society Minister' volunteered was to enquire after my non-government organisation chaperone, whom he told me he had been expecting. When I relayed that they were indisposed at the last minute the knowing, cunning, the *schadenfeudistic* grin that came across his face told me immediately who retained power in this society, notwithstanding the recent purported expansion in civil society freedoms. My chaperone's last-minute absence declared the reality that their life would be at risk if they were to attend the meeting in the ebullience of the supposed-reformist moment only to later find the reforms wound back. Sadly, the glint in the General's eye provided a prescient window onto what was to come. Thankfully, my proposed chaperone now has asylum in another country. The General and Heads of Department and I had a half an hour together in which I canvassed the benefits of an open and free civil society accompanied by a well-resourced, facilitative charity regulator. The General, grinning like the Cheshire cat, left me with instructions to give further detailed information to his assistant, who would attend closely to everything I had to say and relay it to him in detail. For the next forty-five minutes his overwrought associate sat sweating profusely, giving me sympathetic but pained glances that said, 'can you seriously expect that we will implement such reforms? If I advocate for this my own life would be at risk.' Such men had ordered the execution of dissidents with impunity in years past and have returned to that power today. I cannot think of a time that I have encountered the sense of calculated cruelty that I did on that day.

On that same trip I read this verse in the Psalms:

Your foes roared in the place where you met with us;
    they set up their standards as signs.
They behaved like men wielding axes
    to cut through a thicket of trees.

> They smashed all the carved panelling
> with their axes and hatchets.
> They burned your sanctuary to the ground;
> they defiled the dwelling place of your Name.
> They said in their hearts, "We will crush them completely!"
> They burned every place where God was worshiped in the land.[137]

Presenting as it did in the midst of these events, this reading had a profound impact upon me. It seemed to summarise precisely what was happening in that country at that time. My prayer life for that country continually returns to these verses. However, the relevance for the current discussion is that here, again, we see the Bible draw a correspondence between aesthetic beauty and justice – where the Temple invaders 'smashed all the carved panelling with their axes and hatchets', much like the barbaric wrongs being perpetrated on the beautiful people of that country today. In our longing to see the end of such evils it is natural to seek an answer, as Augustine did some seventeen centuries ago, to the question 'what is [evil's] root, and what its seed?'[138]

Augustine's answer to the problem as to how it is that 'I should be gratuitously evil' is simple, but profound in its sublimity. If we ask the question, he writes: 'What is the efficient cause' of the 'evil will?', the answer is: 'there is none.'[139] 'However minutely we examine the case ... we can discern nothing which caused the will of the one to be evil'.[140] Evil is inexplicable. For Augustine 'the evil will ... is not efficient, but deficient'. '[T]o seek to discover the cause ... is as if someone sought to see darkness, or hear silence.'[141] As James KA Smith points out in his commentary on Augustine, if we were to find an efficient cause of evil then evil would make sense. If you can

---

[137] Psalm 74:4-8.
[138] Augustine, 'The Confessions' (n 12) 45, bk 7, ch 5.
[139] Augustine, 'City of God' (n 12) 345, bk 12, ch 6.
[140] Ibid.
[141] Ibid 346, bk 12, ch 7.

locate a cause 'you might even say evil is "natural". But … then it's no longer evil. It's the way things are … You can't protest what is natural; you can't lament what is meant to be … As soon as you "explain" evil it vanishes.'[142] Conversely, to find an efficient cause of evil would subject it to human cogency. We might then run to the opposite conclusion, the false hope of its subjection at human hands. Augustine presents to us the notion of evil as a negation. It is something that arose after God set the default ontological settings of this world. Evil is not part of the divine order. It's inexplicable to us as a result.

Augustine's reasoning complements his separate assertion that the true ontology is that of peace. For many this assertion would seem to run counter to experience. His reasoning warrants some unpacking. In *The City of God* Augustine asserts that all temporal existence longs for peace enjoyed within its frame of reference, which is attained in this world on the completion of conflict.[143] Even the desire for *dominium* is driven by this more primary search for peace:

> How much more powerfully do the laws of man's nature move him to hold fellowship and maintain peace with all men so far as in him lies, since even-wicked men wage war to maintain the peace of their own circle, and wish that, if possible, all men belonged to them, that all men and things might serve but one head, and might, either through love or fear, yield themselves to peace with him! It is thus that pride in its perversity apes God.[144]

Augustine reasons that the 'peace of all things is the tranquillity of order. Order is the distribution which allots things equal and unequal, each to its own place.'[145] By the same principles of peaceful order, 'the discomfort of sickness reveals the pleasure of health' and misery too can be reconciled with peace:

---

[142] James KA Smith, *On the Road with Saint Augustine* (Brazos Press, 2019) 183.

[143] Augustine, 'City of God' (n 12) 376-7, bk 14, ch 1; 387, bk 14, ch 12.

[144] Ibid 517-19, bk 19, ch 12.

[145] Ibid 519-20, bk 19, ch 13.

And hence, though the miserable, in so far as they are such, do certainly not enjoy peace, but are severed from that tranquillity of order in which there is no disturbance, nevertheless, inasmuch as they are deservedly and justly miserable, they are by their very misery connected with order.[146]

The relation of the ontological priority of peace to suffering and evil is then plainly stated: 'true virtue' exists 'when it refers all … that it does in making good use of good and evil things … to that end in which we shall enjoy the best and greatest peace possible.'[147] Augustine thus argued that the role of earthly suffering and sin is to awaken us to the temporality of the earthly order that we might contemplate our final 'end', heaven.[148] Although evil's cause may be inexplicable, the fact that even it has a '*use*'[149] within this temporal order demonstrates its subjection to the ontological priority of peace: 'even what is perverted must of necessity be in harmony with, and in dependence on, and in some part of the order of things, for otherwise it would have no existence at all.'[150] For Augustine, this ontology is eschatological: 'it is by Him the peace of the universe is administered … it is still ruled by the same laws which pervade all things for the conservation of every mortal race, and which brings all things that fit one another into harmony.'[151] The understanding that peace is ontologically basic, as opposed to violence, aids us to see that violence, conflict and injustice are not intrinsic to creation, they are alien.

For those in the midst of suffering Augustine's reasoning, excerpted at its culminating points of inflection as it is above, may appear crass, cold comfort. However, its ramifications are to be properly understood in the full context of Augustine's study of the

---

[146] Ibid.
[147] Ibid 516, bk 19, ch 10.
[148] Ibid.
[149] Ibid 516, bk 19, ch 10 (emphasis added).
[150] Ibid 518, bk 19, ch 12; see also bk 19, chs 4, 10.
[151] Ibid 517-19, bk 19, ch 12.

power of the *domus* (family), of friendship and of *caritas* (charity or love), which are themselves instances of the ontological priority of peace.[152] Within Augustine's understanding can be discerned elements of natural law reasoning and the nascent articulations of the latter doctrine of 'common grace'.[153] That notion holds that, prior to the incursion of evil, God in His abundant love for His created works laced throughout his creation certain default settings intended to bless all humanity. Subsequent to the Fall those settings continue to operate. Their blessing is available to all humanity, regardless of the presence of a personal faith on the part of those who enjoy it. In the final lecture we will return to Augustine to consider the implications he drew from this reasoning for political philosophy.

However, while common grace is available to all, subsequent to the Fall Augustine's mystery of how 'I became evil for no reason' personally implicates us all. As Solzhenitsyn said: 'If only there were evil people somewhere insidiously committing evil deeds, and it were necessary only to separate them from the rest of us and destroy them. But the line dividing good and evil cuts through the heart of every human being.'[154] In *The Brothers Karamazov* Dostoyevsky has Dmitri Karamazov similarly declare 'the horror of it is that beauty is not only a terrifying thing - it is also a mysterious one. In it the Devil struggles with God, and the field of battle is the hearts of men.'[155]

Although our hearts are subject to the mystery of evil, the Bible holds out the great comfort that there remains something irreplace-

---

[152] See, eg, ibid 510-11, bk 19, ch 3; 520, bk 19, ch 14; 522, bk 19, ch 16; 522-3, bk 19, ch 17.

[153] On natural law see, eg, Tom Angier, Iain T Benson and Mark D Retter, *The Cambridge Handbook of Natural Law and Human Rights* (Cambridge University Press, 2022); John Finnis, *Natural Law and Natural Rights* (Oxford University Press, 2nd ed, 2011). On the Calvinist doctrine of common grace see, eg, Kent van Til, 'Subsidiarity and Sphere-Sovereignty' (2008) 69 *Theological Studies* 610; John Halsey Wood Jr, 'Unity and Engagement in the Modern World: Abraham Kuyper's Calvinist Renewal' in Bruce Gordon and Carl R Trueman (eds), *The Oxford Handbook of Calvin and Calvinism* (Oxford University Press, 2021) 508.

[154] Aleksandr Solzhenitsyn, *The Gulag Archipelago* (Collins, 1974) 28.

[155] Fyodor Dostoyevsky, *The Brothers Karamazov*, tr David McDuff (Penguin Books, 1993) 145.

able, something un-dislodgable in the heart of man, something preceding the latterly incursion of evil. As the writer of Ecclesiastes tells us, 'He has also set eternity in the human heart; yet no one can fathom what God has done from beginning to end.'[156] Augustine draws upon similar wells when he states 'our heart is restless until it repose in Thee.'[157] The restless longing Augustine describes, given by God *before* the Fall, prevails notwithstanding the subsequent incursion of inexplicable evil, and notwithstanding our suffering from evil enacted. Our longing for 'that end in which we shall enjoy the best and greatest peace possible'[158] prevails because it is prior to suffering, and prior to the incursion of inexplicable evil. Neither can exhaust it.

The Bible is replete with the promise that this default longing for Him proceeds from a place preceding, and deeper than, our encounter with injustice in this temporal world. The afflicted exiled writer of Lamentations declares his suffering will not deflect him from the certainty that '[b]ecause of the Lord's great love we are not consumed, for his compassions never fail. They are new every morning; great is your faithfulness.'[159] A lawyer with a CLEAR legal aid office recently recounted to me the horrific story of his client, a mother charged with the murder of her own children. Her need for a Saviour preceded the evil in her heart. That need was not exhausted by the evil that she had committed; nor was the evil beyond the bounds of God's love, which she had found in her repentance.

The thought that God's order of peace precedes, and will ultimately prevail against, evil receives a visual representation in Michael Galovic's *September 11 Series/Homage to Fra Angelico*, 2011. Against the backdrop of the crumpled Twin Towers of the World Trade Centre, Galovic's painting expresses the insistent confidence that the risen Christ prevails in His love for humanity. The monstrous horror of the terrorist event is presented to us without re-

---

[156] Ecclesiastes 3:11.
[157] Augustine, 'The Confessions' (n 12) 1, bk 1, ch 1.
[158] Augustine, 'City of God' (n 12) 516, bk 19, ch 10.
[159] Lamentations 3:22-23.

*September 11 Series/Homage to Fra Angelico, 2011,* 70 x 50 cm,
*by Michael Galovic*

serve, depicted in the chaotic, fiery, black, red and grey background.
The confused, swirling backdrop is concentrated on the dark tomb,
with which the charred Towers are associated by their colour. However, in defiance of this depiction of evil in the backdrop, from that
tomb proceeds Christ gently depicted in a posture of meek compas-
sion, to the adoration of those of us surrounding Him. Galovic's picture is striking for its bold, unapologetic affirmation of His Lordship
over inexplicable human evil. The remaining lines of the destroyed
Towers direct our eyes to Christ, whose tender posture in relation
to those surrounding Him tells us that, notwithstanding the horrors

past, the focus of existence remains on God's insistent determination for loving relationship with humanity.

So to summarise, as a theodicy, the Bible, when read with the assistance of Augustine, holds out these three things in which we may hold confidence when encountering injustice:

1. God hates injustice, disclosed in His longing to direct 'the dawn … [to] take the earth by the edges and shake the wicked out of it';

2. Injustice does not prevail against the true and prior ontology of peace, which ontology is to be completely understood when God makes right every wrong in the eschaton where 'He will wipe every tear from' our eyes; and

3. Injustice does not extinguish the more basic human desire for relationship with God, for 'He has also set eternity in the human heart'. This longing, again, signals the reality of the more fundamental ontology of peace.

## The Relation of Art to Injustice

Having established these three things, I want to turn now to consider more closely the relation of injustice to beauty where beauty takes the form of artistic expression. The Sydney-based Bell Shakespeare Company recently put on a production of *King Lear*. Interviewed on ABC Radio National, actor Robert Menzies said that while it had been shunned in prior centuries for its 'unbearable', 'utter cruelty', since the twentieth century *King Lear* has undergone a significant resurgence in popularity.[160] Reflecting a sentiment we have already encountered, he described the play as being 'almost postmodern' on account of the fact that, owing to 'the horrors of the twentieth century and the absurdity of events in that time, people started to make real connections with it.'[161] Critchley sees

[160] 'Bell Shakespeare Enlists Robert Menzies for Titular King Lear Role', *RN Breakfast*, (ABC Radio National, 09 June 2024) https://www.abc.net.au/listen/programs/radionational-breakfast/king-lear-bell-shakespeare/103932836.
[161] Ibid.

a similar continuity between the Ancient Greek plays of Euripides and the insistence of some contemporary playwrights to present us with the cruel injustice of existence:

> Euripides feels so much like our contemporary and the precursor to what we might call the art of the monstrous that we can find in Artaud's Theatre of Cruelty, Hermann Nitsch's blood orgies, or the theatre of Heiner Mueller and, more recently, Sarah Kane. If we look back at much of what is most radical in the art of the last century or so, we can see that we are no longer dealing with an Aristotelian poetics of beauty or even a Kantian analytic of the sublime, but with an art of desublimation that attempts to adumbrate the monstrous, the uncontainable, the unreconciled, that which is unbearable in our experience of reality.[162]

In a similar vein, almost as a harbinger of the morbid sentiments we heard in the early work of TS Eliot and of our contemporary Harry Styles, Anton Chekov ends his famous 1895 play *The Seagull* with a single resounding gunshot, announcing the suicide of the chief protagonist, Konstantin. Chekov's abrupt end to the play leaves his audience in the discomfort of silence, *sans* remedy, reconciliation or hope of redemption. In the terrible dissonance arising in the aftermath of the injustices of the twentieth century, these plays present what Scruton describes as the essence of the aesthetic experience, applied according to a postmodern account: the endeavour to present 'a face-to-face encounter with the world itself, and with the things that it contains, just as we have in the experience of sacred things and sacred places'.[163]

However, if we delve further into the purportedly 'postmodern' works *King Lear* and *The Seagull,* we are struck by the profound exploration of the theme of injustice that they offer. The injustice en-

---

[162] Simon Critchley, *Tragedy, the Greeks, and Us* (Pantheon, 2019) 217.
[163] Scruton (n 50) 132.

countered in *King Lear* is that of a child's ingratitude and of fate. In *The Seagull* it's the injustice that follows narcissistic parenting (which includes the rearing of narcissistic children). These works are post-modern, in the sense that they confront us with the unjust, pointless and absurd brutality of existence as it is. They illustrate how far we have come from Aristotle's 'chief forms of beauty ... order and symmetry and definiteness', from Augustine's proclamation that '[i]n all the arts, that which pleases is harmony'[164] and from the Renaissance art of the ideal. One can readily imagine Nietzsche's commendation of each work for validating his counsel toward *'amor fati'*.[165] In this sense they are postmodern. As Menzies claimed, in light of the horrors of the twentieth century their popularity soars for their willingness to explore the inescapable reality of evil. Ironically, they set out in direct denial of Nietzsche's aphorism that 'we have art lest we perish from the truth'.[166] Rather, these plays are recognised as 'postmodern' precisely for their insistence in pressing upon us the terrifying truth of evil and of injustice.

However, in presenting the face of injustice in such stark relief to us, each play offers its own profound but subtle cry against that injustice. *King Lear* and *The Seagull* both confront us with an invitation to avoid similar tragedies, in the form of the author's gentle critique of the causes of the protagonist's suffering and fall. They can thus be contrasted with Sophocles' play *Oedipus The King*, where the protagonist's tragic fall is without any identifiable fault on his part. The gods command his ruin for actions in which he lacked *mens rea*: his unknowing incest with his mother, and the unwitting murder of his father. For Sophocles our wrestle with fate provides no reasonable explanation for injustice, the gods simply condemn regardless of fault. Extending Critchley's account of Euripides to his contemporary Sophocles, we might then also see in *Oedipus The King* 'the precursor' to the postmodern. As the convul-

---

[164] Augustine (n 29) 19.

[165] Friedrich Nietzsche, *Ecce Homo*, tr Anthony M Ludovici (TN Foulis, 1911) 54.

[166] Nietzsche, *The Will to Power* (n 58) 465, §822.

sions of fate are inexplicable, all that is left to us is Nietzsche's 'formula for greatness in man ... *amor fati*'.[167] However, in the assumption that their protagonist's flaws are scrutable both *King Lear* and *The Seagull* signify a new movement beyond the postmodern. They signal that injustice can be the result of explicable causes, causes we can hold the hope of addressing. In their delicate ways the authors invite us, without direction, to draw our own conclusions on the causes of the protagonist's fall. Roger Scruton writes that in this way the theatre

> involves a reflective study of meanings, and an attempt to find the human significance of the things that appear before us, as they appear. This savouring of impressions leads of its own accord to a critical attitude, and to reason-governed choices. I measure the object observed against the subject observing it and put both in question. This happens when I attend a drama, and respond to the action on stage as though living through it, or when I sit in a tranquil landscape and allow the appearance to seep through my feelings and to become part of me.[168]

In the theatre we are watching ourselves, challenged by what meaning these events may bear for our own actions, motivations or lives. In that sense, Shakespeare and Chekov, as artists, both express a cry for justice – the hope that exposing the human causes of injustice will assist their audience members to avoid such suffering into the future. We might even discern a similar nascent cry subtly underpinning the portraits of modern futility offered by Eliot in *Prufrock* or *Wasteland*, a cry that was to find greater strength in the later work composed after his conversion to Christianity. And so even art that is described as 'postmodern' for its focus on the horrors and banality of existence can transcend postmodernism by affirming our radical and irrepressible need for justice. We are not left solely with the horror, as we are in Greek tragedy. Against the

---

[167] Nietzsche, *Ecce Homo* (n 165) 54.
[168] Scruton (n 50) 131.

horror is expressed a cry for justice. It is a cry which enhances the profound beauty of these *post-post-modern* works. So again, we have found a relation between beauty and justice: these works of art have assumed greater beauty for refusing to forsake the hope of justice in the face of the 'unbearable', 'utter cruelty' of injustice.[169] Notwithstanding postmodernism's best efforts, perhaps Solzhenitsyn's hope in 'that old trinity of Truth, Goodness and Beauty' is not misplaced after all; 'perhaps the fantastic, unpredictable, unexpected stems of Beauty will push through' to confirm to us the reality of justice, of Truth and of Goodness.[170]

## Is Beauty the Biblical Response to Injustice?

Does the Biblical account also assert that beauty is a proper response to injustice? God's response to Job's cry of (what he saw to be) injustice is to direct him to consider the beauty and sublimity of creation. The reply is striking for its simplicity, and perhaps disorienting in its unexpected inimitability. However there is something entirely concordant between God's exhortations to Job to consider the beauty of nature and the great protestation against injustice that accompanies those exhortations, His disclosure that he wants to direct 'the dawn … [to] take the earth by the edges and shake the wicked out of it'.[171] In enfolding His cry for justice within a series of directions to consider the beauty of His creation (directions to regard the dawn, the sea, the stars, the storehouses of snow and the wonder of his creatures and their behaviour, including the Leviathan, lioness, bears, wild ox, ostrich and the horse – all invitations to engage with things of material beauty you will note), God again affirms the Biblical theme encountered in the opening lecture that injustice is unnatural. Injustice defies, is an affront to, the beauty on which He founded this world. It is as unnatural as snow vanishing from its native habitat on the mounts of Lebanon. Injustice inhabits

---

[169] 'Bell Shakespeare Enlists Robert Menzies for Titular King Lear Role' (n 160).
[170] Solzhenitsyn, 'Nobel Lecture in Literature 1970' (n 1) 13.
[171] Job 38:12-13.

with those who would 'smash all the [beautiful] carved panelling [of the Temple] with their axes and hatchets'. Wickedness is, as Augustine's nascent conception of common grace affirms, against the beautiful, natural, peaceful ordering of God's creation. It is a latterly incursion upon the harmonic ordering according to which He set the default settings of this world.

We can say then that, according to a Biblical understanding, there exists a correlation between natural beauty and justice. Just as the woman's act in anointing Jesus is beautiful for its alignment with what is eternally fitting (καλός), so the beautiful snows on the mounts of Lebanon can be a metaphor for a people rightly related to God, and who thus inhabit justice. Expressing the same relation, the destruction of beauty by the invaders who 'smashed all the carved panelling with their axes and hatchets' is offered to emphasise the terrible injustice of the event. According to a Biblical account, justice and beauty are two aspects of God's eternal kingdom that mutually reinforce each other.

## Can the Law be Beautiful?

If there is an alignment between that which God says is beautiful and that which He says is just, we might well then ask whether the law too can be beautiful? A similar enquiry is invited within the tradition of Athens, where Plato expresses the hope that meditation on the beautiful could lead one 'to contemplate and see the beauty of laws and institutions'.[172] From a regard for the classical notion of beauty as a harmonious relation of the parts we might well say that deftly-crafted legal arguments or judicial opinions can be beautiful. Torke discerns within the common law doctrine of precedent the possibility of beauty, where 'each decision may be an embellishment; many together may form a graceful curve, the shape of which seems, from the present, inevitable'.[173] The classical notion that beauty 'holds steadily visible the manifest good of equality and

---

[172]  Plato, 'Symposium' (n 20) 167, §210.
[173]  James W Torke, 'The Aesthetics of Law' (2003) 48 *American Journal of Jurisprudence* 325, 332.

balance'[174] might also find expression within a systematic code of law. Torke argues that '[t]o the extent that such efforts do achieve a sort of completeness and internal consistency, they may be said to achieve elegance and beauty.'[175]

This goal was certainly the aspiration of Enlightenment Reason's first and exemplar attempt at a systematic codification of law, the Napoleonic Code. Leo Tolstoy's *War and Peace* is an inquiry into the 'impossible to understand' 'cause' or 'intense movement' according to which 'millions of Christians killed and tortured each other' during the Napoleonic Wars (the same 'movement' which was to provoke Hegel to formulate his conception of 'the *Geist*').[176] Tolstoy argues that the French self-conception as Europe's liberators, as the bannermen of Enlightenment Reason, was a primary cause of the conflicts. His persistent critique of human hubris is pointedly illustrated by his account of Napoleon Bonaparte's attempts to restore law and order after the fall of Moscow. To make his point Tolstoy extracts from a French letter to the 'tranquil inhabitants of Moscow':

> In respect of philanthropy, the best virtue of monarchs, Napoleon also did all that depended on him. He ordered *Maison de ma Mère* [my mother's house] written on the almshouses, combining in this act a tender filial feeling with the grandeur of a sovereign's virtue. He visited the orphanage [and] allowed the orphans he had saved to kiss his helping hands ...[177]

A legal system such as the Napoleonic Code may be beautiful in that it intends to inspire just or charitable action, as the conquering French letter was intended to show. But as Tolstoy's gentle critique of that letter suggests, the 'beauty' afforded a legal system through

---

[174] Scarry (n 124) 97.

[175] Torke (n 173) 332.

[176] Leo Tolstoy, *War and Peace*, tr Richard Pevear and Larissa Volokhonsky (Vintage Classics, 2009) 604, vol 3, pt 1, ch 1; 823 vol 3, pt 3, ch 1.

[177] Ibid 1005, vol 4, pt 2, ch 9.

its systematic coherence cannot mask its character as a hideous, revolting object in the hands of an unwanted oppressor.

The law may be beautiful, in the sense of its own internal coherence. It may also give rise to beauty, in the sense of providing a framework for just or charitable acts. However, if the law flows from unjust acts, or leads to unjust outcomes, any claim to beauty will fall on deaf ears, just as it did for the defeated Muscovites. While the beauty 'of equality and balance' within a systemised jurisprudence may inspire our regard, if that legal system does not flow from, or result in, just outcomes, any systematic beauty we might have admired will be an affront.

Are we then to conclude that the relation between beauty and justice does not strictly hold? To the contrary, the letter to the Muscovites proves the strength of the relation. Why? Tolstoy is inviting us to the realisation that the apparent 'beauty' of Napoleon's famous systematic legal code is repugnant to those upon whom it enacts oppression. That purported beauty defies the natural alignment between beauty and justice that we have discovered. The Napoleonic Code's purported beauty is an object of revulsion precisely because it makes a claim to beauty that it cannot sustain. By making a false claim to beauty through systematic harmony it has become hideous as an affront to the natural alignment between beauty and justice that we savour. The purported harmonic beauty of a systematic legal code has become odious owing to our prevailing regard for the alignment between beauty and just outcome. Again, we see the depth of the relation between beauty and justice, this time as applied to jurisprudence.

## Postmodernism and the Court

To conclude this second lecture, I will bring these threads together by posing the legal system's distinct role in rebuking postmodernity's claim that truth is relative, and thus, as Nietzsche to Harry Styles tell us, that there is no ultimate truth. These postmodern claims have caused great disruption within our culture. We may think that the culture wars and identity politics are novel phenomena, but in 1970 Solzhenitsyn presciently wrote that 'the message that there are no stable universal concepts of good and evil, that they are all flexible and changing' and 'that therefore you should always act exclusively in the interests of your own party' 'rend and rive our world' and inspire a 'never-ending series of civil wars'.[178] Nevertheless my contention is that the courts, in executing their role in response to the cries of injustice heard at their doorstep, have a definitive role to play in responding to, and prevailing against, postmodernism. My thesis is this: the postmodern assumption that truth is relative to the truth-bearer has been enfolded within the judicial process in a way that ultimately defeats the claims of postmodernism. Let me explain.

Queensland Supreme Court Justice Tom Bradley recently succinctly summarised the process of litigation as being directed to two essential aims. He volunteered: 'There is a simplicity to law. It is concerned with two fundamental questions about human conduct, "What happened?" and "What does it mean?"'[179] As such, a court system is founded upon the understanding that truth is discernible and thus available to answer the victim's cry for justice (whether they be, for example, the victim of a crime or of a contract breach). The procedure of litigation curiously admits of a certain truth in postmodernism. By allowing that both parties will put forward their own version of truth, that both will be self-advancing as an assertion of power, the judicial process shares with postmodernism, indeed seeks to harness, its primary assumptions about human nature. As Charles Dickens famously asserted '[b]ut the mere truth won't do ... You must have a lawyer.'[180]

However, the judicial process, having harnessed postmodernism's insights, does not abandon us to its claim that all assertions of truth are ultimately subjective claims to power. Instead, the adver-

---

[178] Solzhenitsyn, 'Nobel Lecture in Literature 1970' (n 1) 19.

[179] Thomas Bradley, 'Legal History and Human Rights - Reflections on the Revolution' (Lecture, Sir Samuel Griffith Society 34th Conference, 25 May 2024) 2.

[180] Charles Dickens, *Bleak House* (Electric Book Co, 2001) 968.

sarial system proceeds on the hope that, assuming human nature will prefer its own version of truth, in the clash between the parties' self-understanding will be found the actual occurrence. The clash between conflicting accounts will also enable the judge to identify what is the fairest outcome. As Justice Bradley recently summarised:

> As an intellectual exercise, the discipline of law is an analysis of human behaviour. It is perhaps the oldest surviving one. It predates the social sciences, the economic and class based approaches, and their various modernist, post- and post-post-modernist progeny. Past the half-life of those decaying disciplines, the analysis of law continues. This is due to its usefulness in resolving disputes and so allowing relatively peaceful and free societies to continue.[181]

The judicial procedure, as an exercise in the 'analysis of human behaviour', accepts the profundity of the insight that we will see the world from our own perspective. However, the common law adversarial system harnesses this insight in order to ultimately declare upon the objective actuality of the event. The process concludes in agreement with the victim's hope that there is ultimately a fair outcome to be found in objective fact. As Justice Thomas affirms, notwithstanding our post-modern moment, the judicial procedure has not lost the prospect of justice. We should not miss how the system proceeds from a postmodern understanding to ultimately invalidate that understanding. Our court system, by its very operation, proclaims that its processes are sufficient to invalidate the claims of postmodernism.

Torke insightfully argues that there are many parallels between aesthetics and jurisprudence – both 'face the conundrum of the subjective and objective, the particular and general. Both concern human artifacts to which we may apply common interpretive techniques. Suggest[ing] that the objects of both disciplines may

---

[181] Bradley (n 179) 2.

coincide.'[182] But these are means Torke speaks of, not ends. Beyond Torke we have found a further parallel between contemporary post-modern aesthetics and the judicial process. Both engage with the claim that there is no ultimate truth. However, while the judicial process admits that human nature will seek to exert power, and will prefer its own version of truth, it harnesses this insight to ultimately conclude that truth can be found sufficient to triumph over injustice. In resonance with our analysis of Chekov and *King Lear*, the age-old judicial process proves itself to be *post-post-modern*. Moreover, in being what it has always been, it reveals the lack of novelty in post-modernism's insights in order to transcend them (recall that twenty-four centuries before Niertzsche Protagoras theorised that '[m]an ... is the measure of all things, of the existence of things that are, and of the non-existence of things that are not'[183]). The adversarial process of common law justice harnesses, but ultimately collapses, postmodernism's account by declaring that the clash of competing self-interested worldviews can provide a sound basis for determining the just outcome.

In *Law Like Love* WH Auden offers what I conceive to be a delicately phrased summary of my thesis. He takes upon himself to survey the many differing accounts of the law, both natural, and man-made. He tells us that, on one account, 'Law is the wisdom of the old'. He gives us another, perhaps that of natural law:

> Law, say the gardeners, is the sun,
> Law is the one
> All gardeners obey
> To-morrow, yesterday, to-day.

From another perspective, perhaps that of the postmodern legal academic, he writes:

> law-abiding scholars write:
> Law is neither wrong nor right,

---

[182] Torke (n 173) 330.
[183] Plato, 'Theaetetus' (n 20) 517, [152a].

> Law is only crimes
>
> Punished by places and by times

He provides another perspective, perhaps that of the Nietzschean political philosopher:

> Others say, Law is our Fate;
>
> Others say, Law is our State;
>
> Others say, others say
>
> Law is no more,
>
> Law has gone away.

And from another perspective, perhaps that of the democrat:

> And always the very angry crowd,
>
> Very angry and very loud,
>
> Law is We,
>
> And always the soft idiot softly Me.

However, from another perspective, that of the judge sitting on the bench:

> Law, says the judge as he looks down his nose,
>
> Speaking clearly and most severely,
>
> Law is as I've told you before,
>
> Law is as you know I suppose,
>
> Law is but let me explain it once more,
>
> Law is The Law.[184]

Our legal system only assures confidence in the rule of law when the outcome that the judge delivers from the bench aligns (to return to Kant's distinction), not with the *world for us* (the subjective sense of the respective parties), but with the *world as it is* in essence (objective reality). This belief in an objective world is a necessary precondition of the courts' continuing enjoyment of society's confidence that the family on the steps of the courthouse have re-

---

[184] WH Auden, 'Law Like Love' in James Fenton (ed), *The New Faber Book of Love Poems* (Faber and Faber, 2008) 40-1.

ceived the just outcome. As CS Lewis said in *The Abolition of Man*: 'A dogmatic belief in objective value is necessary to the very idea of a rule which is not tyranny'.[185] In exercising their age-old function the courts play a pivotal role in challenging 'the message that there are no stable universal concepts of good and evil, that they are all flexible and changing'. For, as Solzhenitsyn understood, that refrain, if given free rein, will confine human relations to a 'never-ending series of civil wars'.[186]

## Conclusion

Theodore W Adorno famously said 'to write poetry after Auschwitz is barbaric'.[187] Similarly, artists under military dictatorship in Argentina in 1968 considered it 'immoral to make art in the kind of society that existed there.'[188] However, in our exploration of the relation between beauty and justice we have been given compelling evidence across multiple areas of the law that beauty yet continues to fulfil her role in directing us to the reality of truth and the good. We have also come some way in our search for a lawyer's *causa agendi* sufficient to stand in the face of postmodernism's claim that 'we should thrash' the 'philosopher'[189] who claims a relation between the good, the beautiful and the true. In the face of the inexplicable evils of the twentieth century, and postmodernism's resulting ascendancy, we have discovered the great assurance that God retains the desire to, as He disclosed to Job, direct 'the dawn ... [to] take the earth by the edges and shake the wicked out of it'. This has led us to observe the Biblical correlation between natural beauty and justice. We have also taken heart that injustice and evil do not extinguish the more-basic, God-implanted human desire to find our heart's rest in Him. We have seen the beauty of a seemingly 'postmodern' work

---

[185] Lewis, *The Abolition of Man* (n 45) 46.

[186] Solzhenitsyn, 'Nobel Lecture in Literature 1970' (n 1) 19.

[187] Theodore W Adorno, *Prisms*, tr Samuel Weber and Shierry Weber (MIT Press, 1967) 34.

[188] Gablik (n 60) 26.

[189] Nietzsche, *The Will to Power* (n 58) 465, §822.

of art enhanced through its expression of the radical human cry for justice in the face of postmodernity's depiction of the horrors, banality and meaninglessness of existence. We have seen how both popular culture and the law are (perhaps unwittingly) embroiled in the mêlées of the philosophy of modernity. I have argued that the judicial process harnesses the postmodern conception of human nature to ultimately prevail against that conception. From these understandings a theory of the distinct role we lawyers might play in facing the evil this temporal world presents is beginning to take shape. The third talk in this series will address this role under the title 'Beauty, the Lawyer and Creativity'. We will consider how our creative efforts as professionals might seek to give effect to CS Lewis' insight that: 'If you read history, you will find that the Christians who did the most for the present world were just those who thought most of the next.'[190]

## Lecture 2 Discussion Questions

1. Do you agree that beauty has a role to play in reply to injustice?

2. How do you seek to serve those who have been the victims of injustice? How can beauty play a role in this?

3. How might your work participate in God's desire to give orders to 'the dawn … [to] take the earth by the edges and shake the wicked out of it'.

4. In what ways can you conceive of your own work as creating beauty?

5. Do you agree that the courts have a role to play in reply to postmodernism?

---

[190] CS Lewis, *Mere Christianity* (Pomodoro Books, 2020) 111.

# LECTURE 3

# *Beauty, the Lawyer and Creativity*

## Creatives as Recanting Lawyers

One does not need to venture far into the Australian comedy circuit before stumbling over a recanting lawyer. One (possibly whimsical) Australian study reports that 47% of Australian comedians have either studied or practised law.[191] We have Steve Vizard, Jane Turner, Rebel Wilson, Shaun Micallef, Charlie Pickering, Anh Do, four members of The Chaser, and members of the D-Generation, including various of the writers of that classic Australian movie, *The Castle*. On my brief investigation, the United Kingdom can claim John Cleese, Susan Calman and Clive Anderson. Having surveyed this list of luminaries, one might wonder whether the law compels a particular strand of black humour. What is it about lawyering that makes it so apparently ripe with potential to produce hard-nosed cynicism toward politics and society?

Beyond comedians, who I am content to call 'artists', there are many other creatives who have escaped their lawyer pasts. Charles Dickens had a particularly unflattering view of lawyers and the law, informed by his time working as a young solicitor's clerk. He wrote in *The Old Curiosity Shop*: 'It is a pleasant world we live in, sir, a very pleasant world. There are bad people in it, Mr. Richard, but if there were no bad people, there would be no good lawyers.'[192] With similar cynicism he wrote: 'The one great principle of English law is to make business for itself.'[193] However, other creatives, thankfully, emerged from their early encounter with the law unscathed by this

---

[191] Gav George, 'Rise of the Law-medians: Lawyers Drop Out to Become Comedians', *enhancentertainment* <https://enhancentertainment.com.au/blog/rise-of-law-medians-lawyers-drop-out-become-comedians/>.

[192] Charles Dickens, *The Old Curiosity Shop* (Open Road Media Integrated Media, 2015) 331.

[193] Dickens, *Bleak House* (n 180) 755.

seemingly characteristic cynicism. Wassily Kandinsky moved from study of the law to painting after a transformative encounter with beauty, inspired by the release of Claude Monet's *Haystacks* and by Richard Wagner's opera *Lohengrin*. Novelist and poet Sir Walter Scott, also a recanting lawyer, famously wrote: 'A lawyer without history or literature is a mechanic, a mere working mason; if he possesses some knowledge of these, he may venture to call himself an architect.'[194]

In these final two lectures we will turn to consider how we lawyers may be architects. We are going to make an attempt at a practical application of the things we have been studying. We will explore how our creativity may make a contribution to our clients, and to wider society. In this third lecture, we will consider what implications a love of beauty may have for a Christian lawyer in their day-to-day practice. Although we have in view the practicing lawyer, policy-maker and legislator in particular (being the audience of the original lectures), the discussion is of equal relevance to all who would wish to more completely direct their talent to the common good through the service of others. We will first consider the creative process, before turning to how that process may arrest our *métier*. In the final lecture we will put this framework to work by considering how an understanding of history, particularly intellectual history, may make us architects by informing our contribution to the common good.

## Lawyers and the 'Human Drive for Beauty'

Notwithstanding that these eminent recanting-lawyer artists felt the need to eschew their lawyer's garbs in pursuit of creativity, the heart of the practicing lawyer is not immune from what NT Wright calls 'our human drive for beauty, for transcendent meaning'. Wright interprets this human instinct as being 'God-given: a signpost, designed to lead us back to his presence'. In his study of the Gospel of John, Wright observes that:

---

[194] Walter Scott, *Guy Mannering* (EP Dutton & Company, 1908) ch 37.

By focusing our attention, in his telling of Jesus's story, on the Tabernacle and Temple as well as the world of creation, John was picking up their ultimate purpose: to point forward to the coming day when, with the Word having become flesh, beauty itself would become incarnate to make all things new. We cannot, then, get all the way by argument alone from the human perception and enjoyment of beauty to the existence or character of the Creator. But when, not least through the literary beauty of John's gospel, we are confronted with the beauty of redeeming love in the story of Jesus, we realize, looking back, that the signals we were receiving from all the beauty in the world were telling the truth.[195]

Echoing the thoughts of CS Lewis and of GK Chesterton that we encountered in the first lecture, Wright claims that:

We are all of us hardwired for beauty, searching for a deeper and richer meaning in a world that sometimes seems to overflow with delight but at other times feels dreadful and cold. Beauty - the haunting sense of loveliness, the transient yet utterly powerful stabs of something like love but something more and different as well - is not after all a mere evolutionary twist, an echo of an atavistic urge to hunt prey, to find a mate, or to escape danger. It is a pointer to the strange, gently demanding presence of the living God in the midst of his world.[196]

If we are all 'hardwired for beauty' perhaps even we cynical, hardened lawyers may yet hold onto the legitimate hope of exploring and expressing 'our human drive for beauty, for transcendent meaning' within our day to day practice. If, as Wright asserts, this drive is 'God-given: a signpost, designed to lead us back to his presence' it is, like Augustine's 'restless'[197] heart, immutable within us.

---

[195] Wright (n 22) 31.
[196] Ibid 27.
[197] Augustine, 'The Confessions' (n 12) 1, bk 1, ch 1.

In this third lecture I want to explore how this God-given love for beauty and creativity may be put to use for our clients. To do this I will develop a Christian philosophy of beauty in response to the Enlightenment separation of object and subject that we encountered in the opening lecture. I will apply this philosophy to the life of the practicing lawyer, demonstrating its sufficiency to ground, motivate and order our many disparate efforts toward the common good.

## The Creative Urge as a Process

So, let's begin by considering how we lawyers can draw upon this God-given desire for beauty. How might we lawyers engage in the creative process within the grind of our day to day practice? And most importantly, how could this engagement possibly be a signpost to the truth that, as Wright has it, 'beauty itself [has] become incarnate to make all things new'? Let's then take a short excursion into the creative urge as a process; the process of the aesthete. Mozart wrote in a letter to a friend of musical ideas coming to him

> in a stream ... [I] keep them in my head, and people say I often hum them over to myself. Well, if I can hold onto them, they begin to join on to one another, as if they were bits a pastry cook should join together in the pantry. And now my soul gets heated, and if nothing disturbs me, the piece grows larger and brighter until, however long it is, it is all finished at once in my mind, so that I can now see it at a glance as if it were a pretty picture or a pleasing person. Then I don't hear the notes one after the other, as they are hereafter to be played, but it is as if in my fancy they were all at once.[198]

Does your fashioning of legal argument, your solution-finding for your client engage in a similar process, comprised of sudden moments of inspiration followed by an Aristotelian / Augustinian effort at harmonisation and synthesisation?

---

[198] Wolfgang Amadeus Mozart quoted in Gallant (n 29) 19.

What then might the process of creative lawyering look like? What is your method of creative inspiration? Do your best solutions arise when working individually, in a group, or both, depending on the nature of the differing Gordian knots you seek to untie? I recall one of the earliest things to strike me for its novelty in the practice of law was my second managing partner Matthew Turnour's insight that the lawyer exists to find creative solutions that no one else sees. As a freshly minted lawyer it had never occurred to me that the law was a framework for enabling creativity. I had, like many lawyers, perhaps unwittingly begun with a conception of the law as inherently prescriptive; determinative of a limited set of options requiring absolute compliance. What Matthew demonstrated for me is that a lawyer can be abundantly creative, indeed should be so, precisely because the law, properly understood, operates as a scaffolding framework for permissible action. Within that legal architecture a myriad of possible solutions present for a client. The task of the lawyer practicing his craft with excellence is to have an understanding of the law that is of sufficient depth to enable the identification of that myriad.

What is your creative process? Mine is much like Mozart's pastry cook. When drafting advices, I will have moments of inspiration and hasten to jot them down before they elude me. Once the full tableau of ideas is before me, I will seek harmonisation and synthesis. Further, when formulating solutions within my practice, I will intentionally state to the lawyers in the firm and even to clients, that in order to attain to the best outcome I will proactively propose some certain ideas, bounce potential solutions around and seek to winnow out any unforeseen consequences in order to land upon proof-tested solutions. I clarify that I am seeking to converse with both their initial reactions and the subsequent reactions that emerge with the benefit of reflection. Universally I find that seeking the insight of others creates and inspires my own ability to provide insight.

There is a current debate within psychological schools as to the respective strengths of cultural creativity and individual creativity.[199] One of the lead protagonists on the side of cultural creativity, Mihaly Csikszentmihalyi focusses on how certain cultural conditions can create an atmosphere that inspires creativity. He points to Renaissance Florence where the wealthy were encouraged to advertise their prosperity and power through art, which in turn attracted artists, sculptors and architects and inspired an irrepressible culture of creativity and innovation.[200] The realisation that a group of people can develop a culture imbued with creative energy is of great relevance to the leader of a law firm, whose ambition, rightly ordered (imbibing Augustine's definition of 'virtue [as] the order of love'[201]), should include the raising up of the next generation of creative, solution finding lawyers. It is a truth equally applicable to all the service-oriented vocations.

## The Christian Lawyer and the Creative Process

If we accept that the lawyer is engaged in a creative process, what then does the artist have to teach the lawyer about that process? For American Christian philosopher Nicholas Wolterstorff, *the audience that the artist has in view* is the decisive consideration within the creative process. He asks:

> does the composer make his evaluations and choices by reference to what he expects will give greater satisfaction to anticipated audiences? … for the most part, he evaluates and chooses as he does because he wants to compose a good sonata. He chooses this sound-pattern over that one because he thinks it makes for a better sonata. Sometimes he may be able to identify what it is about this sound-pattern that makes it better than that one, and often he will not be able to do so. He senses that it is better but isn't able to say why.[202]

---

[199] Les Jones, 'Plaiting Gravy' (2023) 153 *Philosophy Now* 8, 11.

[200] Mihaly Csikszentmihalyi, *Flow and the Foundations of Positive Psychology: The Collected Works of Mihaly Csikszentmihalyi* (Springer Netherlands, 2014) 296.

[201] Augustine, 'City of God' (n 12) 416, bk 15, ch 22.

[202] Nicholas Wolterstorff, 'Beauty and Justice' (2009) 73(4) *The Cresset* 6.

Wolterstorff asserts that the proper audience of the artist is the artist herself. The central consideration of the creative process is the authentic representation of the emotion, the concept, the inclination, of the insight that the artist seeks to convey. On Wolterstorff's conception of the creative process, the concerns of the audience outside of the artist are secondary to the goal of authentic self-representation.

In contrast, the central audience of the lawyer's imaginative efforts, according to our legal duty of loyalty, is the client. Yet this other-focus does not mean we lawyers are engaged in an exercise that is in any sense less creative than that of the artist. Our creative process, our effort at fashioning solutions for those we serve, is different precisely because we have an external audience in view. We are not simply seeking to express a conjunction of subject and object, as the Romantics were. In the prior lecture we heard that harmony and coherence in jurisprudence or even legal argumentation can be expressive of beauty. In seeking to fashion coherent legal arguments or inventive solutions that comprehend our client's unique needs and constraints, we seek to create beauty and harmony, as it were, for, or on the part of, others.

RG Collingwood, described as 'the greatest British philosopher of history of the twentieth century',[203] argued that 'the aesthetic experience, or artistic activity, is the experience of expressing one's emotions; and that which expresses them is the total imaginative activity called indifferently language or art. This is art proper.'[204] For Collingwood 'true art, as opposed to mere entertainment, constructs an "imaginary object" which can be shared, as an idea can be, by the artist with his public. In looking at a painting or listening to a symphony ... we must imaginatively reconstruct the artist's own creative thought.'[205] His belief, drawn from his work as a historian,

---

[203] Simon Blackburn, 'Collingwood, Robin George', Concise Routledge Encyclopaedia of Philosophy (Routledge, 2000) 148.

[204] RG Collingwood, The Principles of Art (Clarendon Press, 1938) 275.

[205] Michael Wreen, 'Collingwood, Robin George' in Ted Honderich (ed), Oxford Companion to Philosophy (Oxford University Press, 1995) 141.

was that the process of comprehending 'the interpretation of others [as expressed in their art] was not a scientific exercise of fitting their behaviour into a network of generalisations but a matter of rethinking their thoughts for oneself'.[206] The notion that art presents an invitation to 'rethink' the artist's thought for ourselves is of immense relevance to the lawyer, who is compelled by her craft to walk in the shoes of her client.

One of the shrewdest commendations I have received from a client was that I was able to explain the conjunction of the complicated world of the law (in that case managed investment schemes, financial services licencing, property management and charitable endorsements) with their unique purpose and circumstance, while fashioning *with them* solutions that enabled freedom to move within the strictures of the regime while maintaining fidelity to their distinct character and ethos. In this sense, the successful lawyer is a true empath, he must be able to understand the constraints of the client and the outcomes that they seek and, in light of the law, harmonise these factors within a solution that is the client's own. This exercise is, at its heart, a creative process, as RG Collingwood has it, 'a matter of rethinking [the client's] thoughts for oneself'.[207] Note also that, at its heart, the lawyer's creative process is a collective, not individual, one. It is engaged in *with* the client.

Just as we would like to think that Wolterstorff's composer is choosing the option that better expresses or is coherent with, the message *she seeks* to convey, being an authentic representation of her own emotion, concept, inclination, or insight, so the lawyer seeks to find a coherent harmonised framework that most ably expresses the concerns, worldview and ambition of *her client*. I think we rightly consider this to be a work of beauty. Again, this is a truth that is applicable to all the service-oriented vocations. For the lawyer the beauty of this creative process is only *enhanced* through the *requirement* that it be other-focussed, in accordance with our duty

---

[206] Blackburn (n 203) 148.
[207] Ibid.

of loyalty to our clients. In the discussion questions that accompany this lecture you will be given the opportunity to reflect upon whether this has, or could into the future, provide an accurate description of the creative process that you engage in when you seek to serve others in your professional life.

Within contemporary aesthetics the question 'who comprises the proper audience?' is a key axis upon which the value of aesthetic art is determined. The differing answers ventured to that question distinguish the differing schools within contemporary philosophical debate. The first school is represented by Solzhenitsyn and Gablik, who emphasise the social role of beauty, where the audience is *the other*, upon whom the artist seeks to impress a certain truth or good. For Wolterstorff and for RG Collingwood the proper audience for art is that art's own author. To that extent, they thus imbibe the self-focussed spirit of modern art critiqued by Gablik, in which 'to know oneself becomes an end, instead of a means through which one knows the world.'[208] On the modernist conception of art, the artist is the ultimate intended beneficiary. The goal of the artistic work is to express a certain emotion, inclination or insight that is enlightening *to the artist*.

This individualist account of creative value accentuates for us the unique distinctive, and beauty, of the lawyer's particular form of creativity: it is always other-focussed. It seeks to enable creative solutions *for others*, empathetically aware of their own strictures and hopes, including those they may not have yet identified for themselves. The same basic virtue of other-focussed creativity lies at the heart of the work of the policy-maker and legislator, who also must refine their abilities as empaths. This makes the solution-finding process of the lawyer (in which descriptor we have included the policy-maker and legislator) none the less creative than the forms of art that Wolterstorff or Collingwood have in view. Given that insight, discernment, empathy and wisdom are necessary virtues for this creative process, and given that these character traits

---

[208] Gablik (n 60) 24.

are all esteemed in Scripture, we might have reason to hope that the Christian lawyer, relying on Christ, displays a unique potential to be distinguished for excellence in this domain.

In exploring this theme of the centrality of the audience to aesthetic value, I also want to suggest that for the Christian lawyer there are two additional and unique distinctives that present in the creative process. Returning to the story of the woman who anointed Jesus with burial oil considered in the opening lecture, when the Christian lawyer seeks to create something of beauty, they are ambitious to hear Jesus' affirmation that 'you have done a beautiful thing to me'. Although operating with the duty of loyalty firmly in view, underpinning all of our service to clients lies the awareness that we are playing to an audience of One. Recall that the woman's actions, which Jesus saw as beautiful, were misunderstood and rebuked by others present. She was, however, firmly focussed on playing to the audience of One. Whether the creative efforts we undertake for clients actually create beauty is ultimately determined against a measure authored by Him. He pronounces upon the final measure of beauty. The woman with burial oil tells us that we are to have our sole care toward whether He will see intrinsic worth in our service for clients. How fitting that Christ would celebrate this model of single-minded devotion with the promise 'that wherever the gospel is preached throughout the world, what she has done will also be told, in memory of her.'[209]

The second distinctive that I want to draw out as unique to the Christian lawyers' creative process is the Bible's audacious claim that an encounter with God will inspire an upwelling of creativity in which God Himself exercises agency. The Bible is replete with examples affirming that an upwelling of creative expression is the natural response for those who encounter God's beauty. Consider the very first act of the Israelites after travelling through the Red Sea:

---

[209] Matthew 26:13.

the composition of a poem sung corporately.[210] Hannah's response of gratitude to God's kindness in gifting her a child was expressed in poetic verse, as was Mary's Magnificat[211] and Zechariah's joy at seeing his son John the Baptist.[212] Simeon also broke into poetic verse on holding the Saviour child.[213] In John's account of the final days, the sight of the slain lamb found worthy to open the 'scroll and its seven seals' provokes the twenty-four human elders to combine with 'the four living creatures' in offering '*a new song*'.[214]

The Bible affirms not only that the personal knowledge of God's intervention will inspire creativity, it also confirms that God Himself can partner with us in that creativity. The garments of the priests who will serve at the Temple are to be made by 'all the skilled workers *to whom I have given wisdom*'.[215] *His wisdom* enlivens *their creativity*. Psalm 45 offers a similar study in the creative process inspired by God's beauty. Looking upon God's anointed King, the Psalmist writes:

> My heart is stirred by a noble theme
>> as I recite my verses for the king;
>> my tongue is the pen of a skilful writer.

The Psalmist suggests that his creative inspiration is a gift of God when he acknowledges the beauty of 'lips' that 'have been anointed with grace'.[216] What is distinctive about Christianity's claim, and what makes it an object of scorn, is the audacious assertion that through belief in the death and resurrection of Jesus Christ one might then attain to a real relationship with the Creator of the Universe. The Psalmist tells us that it is that relationship that is the well-spring of beauty. It is also what the woman with burial oil tells us; she alone

---

[210] Exodus 15.
[211] 1 Samuel 2:1-10; Luke 1:46-55.
[212] Luke 1:67-79.
[213] Luke 2:28-32.
[214] Revelation 5 (emphasis added).
[215] Exodus 28:3 (emphasis added).
[216] Psalm 45:1-2.

among those present understood what Jesus would see as beautiful and she alone acted to produce its realisation. In so doing, she
showed that the production of artifacts of beauty proceed from our
distinct and personal understanding of, and relationship, with Jesus.

## A Christian Philosophy of Beauty

This Biblical account of creativity now positions me to present a
Christian Philosophy of Beauty. As I will argue, it is a philosophy
that has unique bearing in our search for a coherent *causa agendi*
for the lawyer; for a theoretical framework sufficient to motivate
and order her otherwise many disparate efforts toward the common good. The story of the woman with burial oil tells us that the
measure of the intrinsic worth of our creative efforts and their result is proclaimed by no other than Christ himself. He alone saw in
the woman's actions something 'beautiful'. Notice that in that single
proclamation Christ confirms both that beauty exists in the objective *world as it is*, and also in our subjective appreciation of it, the
*world for us*. Defying Nietzsche's desire to 'thrash' those who would
assert the reality of beauty, He confirms that both objective beauty
and our subjective appreciation of it can exist in perfect alignment.
For the Christian this settles the modern contention over what is
beautiful, encountered in the first lecture when considering the sub-
ject/object divide and the problem of our relation to the absolute.
The pronouncement of what is 'beautiful' proceeds from the author
of beauty Himself, from the author of the sunset, from the creator of
the remote Cumbrian waterfall. Beauty is not in the eye of the postmodern beholder; it is in His eye. He has the authority to declare
its presence, including in the woman's act of anointing His body.
The story of the woman with burial oil stands for authority that we
humans can have an accurate subjective appreciation of objective
beauty *as it is*.

In declaring that Christ, as the author of creation,[217] determines
objective beauty, the story of the woman with burial oil signifies

---

[217] Colossians 1:16-17.

the Christian's departure from Kant's and postmodernism's contention that we may never apprehend true objective reality. From the
woman's story we are clearly to understand that objective beauty
exists. We are further to understand that that beauty can be accu-
rately appreciated within our subjective understanding. That is, the
Bible holds out the expectation that our subjective understanding
will apprehend beauty as it objectively is. The profound importance
of this realisation is confirmed by Christ's pronouncement that all
future generations will hear His declaration that her act was beautiful. Christ intended that 'wherever the gospel is preached' all future
generations would have the opportunity to appreciate the beauty in
her actions.

In the story of the woman with burial oil Christ, as God, as the
creator of objective beauty, declared His prerogative to pronounce
upon beauty. We might even say that Christ, as a human, Himself
engaged in a subjective appreciation of the objective beauty of her
act. But we can go further than this. Christ, as God, but also as
perfectly man, perfectly merges the object and the subject in His
declaration that 'she has done a beautiful thing to me'. The story of
the woman shows us the extent to which Kant's disjunction of the
subjective world of perception from an unknowable objective world
of reality departs from a Biblical understanding. In Christ, God, as
man, perfectly combines the object and the subject in his declaration that the woman's act of service was beautiful. (As an aside, we
might pause to consider that, if we admit that the relation between
beauty and the good underpins Jesus' response to the woman (as
argued in the first lecture),[218] that declaration, proceeding from the
author of creation, would also call into question Kant's contention
that morality is universal and discernible to human reason without
the need for divine revelation.)

The Protestant philosopher Johann Georg Hamann, a one-time
drinking buddy of Kant's, a scathing critic of Kant's account of
reason, but also the organiser of the first publication of Kant's *The*

---

[218]  See pages 8 to 9.

*Critique of Judgement*, wrote: 'All the colours of this most beautiful world grow pale once you extinguish its light, the firstborn of creation.'[219] Writing in his commentary on Hamann, John R Betz argues 'it is now clear that the key to a full-blooded aesthetics is Christ. ... Whereas without Christ we can neither fully see nor fully feel, with Christ "the more we are able to see and taste and behold and touch His loving condescension ... in his creatures."'[220] As Psalm 45 confirms, God enlivens our ability to both appreciate and make beauty. Hamann returns us to the truth that we encountered in the first lecture when considering the Old Testament Temple as a signification of the worth that God places upon material beauty. In its beauty, the Temple, like the Garden of Eden, also signifies that God intended, as a facet of our human condition, that our subjective appreciation would delight in objective beauty *as it is*. It also returns us to the opening lecture's four illustrations of how the Judeo-Christian conception of nature as a created work leads us to the necessity of beauty to human fulfilment. In these myriad ways the Biblical account confirms that beauty is objectively real, and that we are right in thinking we may subjectively enjoy it *as it is*. The significance of the story of the woman with burial oil for our investigation is found in His declaration that the subjective and the objective are united. In this proclamation He reclaims what the Enlightenment and its progeny postmodernism eschewed, what the Romantics sought and what indigenous societies retain.

## Implications for our Vocation

It remains to bring this Christian philosophy of beauty back to the world of the practicing lawyer. I want to argue that this account of the Christian philosophy of beauty offers a *causa agendi* sufficient to enable action by the Christian lawyer. Indeed, it provides a motiva-

---

[219] Johann Georg Hamann, *Writings on Philosophy and Language*, tr Kenneth Haynes (Cambridge University Press, 2007) 78.

[220] John R Betz, *After Enlightenment: The Post-Secular Vision of JG Hamann* (Oxford Wiley-Blackwell, 2009) 133 quoting Johann Georg Hamann, in Josef Nadler (ed), *Sämtliche Werke* (Herder, 1949-57) vol 2, 207.

tion for action that applies equally to all those who seek meaning within their chosen line of work. NT Wright offers this account of the artist:

> To make sense of and celebrate a beautiful world through the production of artifacts that are themselves beautiful is part of the call to be stewards of creation, as was Adam's naming of the animals. Genuine art is thus itself a response to the beauty of creation, which itself is a pointer to the beauty of God.[221]

This description of the artist is equally true of the Christian lawyer or professional seeking to fashion solutions (*qua* artifacts) for her client that respond to their unique need, drawing upon the inspiration of the Holy Spirit.

In that effort, the woman with burial oil assists us to see that the ultimate goal in our *métier* is a single-minded ambition to hear Him say 'you have done a beautiful thing to me'. That is an ambition to fashion and appreciate works of beauty, *as it is*. When we twenty-first century professionals have the single ambition of performing an act expressing objective beauty, of revealing reality, the worth of that beautiful creation, in reality, is proclaimed by Christ. In that proclamation Christ discloses His intention that we attain to a subjective appreciation of the objectively beautiful act created. In this, the objective and subjective find perfect alignment, because they emanate from the author of beauty, in whom subjective and objective beauty are truly and originally aligned. In the subjective appreciation of objective beauty, the lawyer-creator and Christ are joined.

This account of beauty has weighty implications for those lawyers who are committed to justice. It posits that we Christian lawyers have two audiences: the client, to whom we have our duty of loyalty, and Him, from whom all beauty flows. In the preceding lecture we explored the Biblical correlation between natural beauty and jus-

---

[221] Wright (n 22) 32.

tice against the backdrop of assertions that there is a relation between beauty, the true and the good. When we lawyers pray 'your
kingdom come, your will be done, on earth as it is in heaven',[222] we
are asking to be aligned with His desire to 'take the earth by the
edges and shake the wicked out of it'.[223] Given the *métier* that accompanies His desire for justice, in this prayer we might well see
ourselves enjoying the territory described by Christ when He said
'I am the vine; you are the branches. If you remain in me and I in
you, you will bear much fruit.'[224] The lawyer who conceives of her
creative acts in service of her clients as rendering beauty expresses
a unique hope in the attainment of justice, *as it is*.

## Beauty as Suffering and the Christian Lawyer

Having come this far, we should not miss the *particular form* of
beauty that Jesus endorses in the actions of the woman. It is one
that has immense consequence for the lawyer seeking a theoretical
framework to ground their action toward the common good. Not
only does Jesus' acclamation of the woman's act of service affirm
the *existence* of objective beauty, it also directs us to the *content* of
that eternal beauty. As we saw in the first lecture, her act, itself one
of humble service, was an act of beauty (καλός) precisely because
it was in pleasant alignment with what was eternally fitting for that
moment. By preparing Jesus for His burial the intrinsic beauty of
her act was found in its direction to the ultimate service offered for
us: His suffering on the Cross.

Suffering inhabits a sacred place within the Christian tradition.
Those among us that serve the suffering are in a privileged position.
Recall Jesus' statement that '[t]ruly I tell you, whatever you did for
one of the least of these brothers and sisters of mine [the hungry, the
thirsty, the stranger, the sick, the imprisoned], you did for me.'[225] The

---

[222] Matthew 6:10.
[223] Job 38:12-13.
[224] John 15:5.
[225] Matthew 25:40.

example of the woman with burial oil reveals a Christian's humble service for the broken to be an act of intrinsic beauty, as defined by the author of beauty Himself. When in the line of our vocation we serve clients who are suffering, we can take heart that we are serving Christ. Returning to Solzhenitsyn's thesis that beauty is the way to preserve the good and the true in response to injustice, the story of the woman affirms that the Christian lawyer's act of sacrifice for the suffering expresses a form of beauty that is coherent with what is eternally good and true. The same is true of all those called to serve the suffering through their *métier*. In a further gospel account involving the washing of feet Jesus tells us:

> Now that I, your Lord and Teacher, have washed your feet, you also should wash one another's feet. I have set you an example that you should do as I have done for you. Very truly I tell you, no servant is greater than his master, nor is a messenger greater than the one who sent him. Now that you know these things, you will be blessed if you do them.[226]

There is a happy correspondence between Jesus' modelling of the Christian life as one of service and the requirement that lawyers (in which we include policy-makers and legislators) be, at their heart, servants.[227]

The profound exceptionality of Christ's lauding of humble sacrifice is illustrated by (what is possibly) that most distinct human inclination, also prompted by suffering: *schadenfreude*, the curious human inclination toward delight in the misfortune of others. Philosophers have long puzzled over the complex psychology of *schadenfreude*, found in its mixture of revulsion, fascination, comfort and delight. Our delight and comfort stem from the fact that we ourselves are not the subject of the suffering we observe. But while *schadenfreude* takes comfort in the avoidance of suffering, its revul-

---

[226] John 13:14-17.
[227] Mark 10:35-45.

sion and fascination speak to our own awareness of our vulnerability to fate. The Bible does not avoid encountering this worst of human predispositions. That *schadenfreude* presents as the polar opposite of the Bible's ambition for humanity is illustrated by its presentation at the very moment of the seeming triumph of the forces of darkness, in the insults hurled at the dying Christ by passers-by.

The first conversation between real-life lawyers I can recall overhearing as a young undergraduate remains with me not for the nobility of the protagonists' commitment to their suffering clientele, but rather for the picture of uninhibited *schadenfreude* it presented. In a courtroom in country New South Wales I was amazed to overhear two lawyers laughing cynically with mutual gratification over the agreed stupidity of their client's actions. It was clear that the stories they were exchanging were just the latest iteration within a long-running dialogue of mutual *schadenfreudistic* delight. Lawyers have a terrible (and sometimes deserved) reputation for their cold hearts and cheerless cynicism. That cynicism is in part explicable when it is understood as fuelled by the lawyers' perpetual encounter with the tragic (perhaps also illustrating the fertile breeding ground the law provides for the recanting lawyer-cum-comedians we encountered at the beginning of this lecture). Alongside pride, *schadenfreude* could well be a contender for the prize of 'the besetting sin of the lawyer'. However, as the story of the woman with burial oil signifies, rather than the all-too human reaction of delight in the suffering of others, we Christian lawyers have the privilege of exhibiting to the world the precisely antithetical reaction; that which Christ has declared to be beautiful: humble, self-sacrificing service of the suffering.

It was in the physical and temporal event of the Cross, the ultimate expression of His love, that God chose the experience of suffering to express His complete association with our humanity. Our basic intuition would tell us that there is no state of existence which is more separated from a perfect God than suffering. After all, as God says, the result of the Fall is 'curse' and 'painful toil'.[228] We might well say suffering is the characteristic human condition consequent

---

[228] Genesis 3:17.

upon the Fall. The understanding of suffering as the definitive human experience explains why God chose the moment of the Cross as the perfect culmination of His desire for complete affinity with humanity. Suffering, a phenomenon definitive of human experience, is the experience in which God ultimately completes His affinity with us. Suffering thus has immense worth in the Christian narrative. In the Cross God chose to invade and to overcome the very experience that characterises our state subsequent to our departure from Him in the Garden of Eden. In inhabiting suffering God expressed the ultimate fulfilment of His love and association with us. His affinity for the suffering has lost none of its power to this day and can be expressed through the actions of a Christian lawyer in service of her clients.

However, precisely because the archetype of the *schadenfreudistic* lawyer remains so prevalent, as typified by those cynical lawyers in that country courtroom, Shakespeare's seventeenth century exhortation '[l]et's kill all the lawyers'[229] has today lost none of its gleeful resonance. Notwithstanding the mirthful, and at times not so mirthful, ire directed toward the legal profession, it is also true that suffering can be a feature of the lawyer's life. The escalated levels of depression and substance abuse amongst the profession are concomitants of the pressures and privileges it entails. When considering the application of the theme of suffering for the lawyer, it is necessary that we also make mention of the reality of those who have suffered in the service of the law. This suffering can involve the injustice of a slander on one's reputation where the obligation of confidentiality precludes a response. The lawyer who spends hours spent on a pro bono matter only to have the client ignore your advice or, worse, sue you alleging negligence also suffers. Lawyers

---

[229] William Shakespeare, 'Henry VI', *The Complete Works of William Shakespeare* (Rock Point, 2014) 55, Part 2, Act 4, Scene 2. The frequent quoting of this phrase misunderstands Shakespeare's reference. The rebels in Henry VI knew they would have to 'kill all the lawyers' to upend the law and usher in their revolutionary vision. Shakespeare intended this as a compliment to lawyers. I am indebted to Keith Thompson for drawing this to my attention.

can also personally suffer on account of the weight of the decisions placed upon them, or the hours lost to family and loved ones, or the betrayal of a business partner, the list goes on. Owing to our duties of loyalty and confidentiality some of the suffering we experience will only be known in eternity. It is the nature of our obligations of confidentiality that not even our spouse can know the extent of the challenges that present to us. It has however been my experience that the acts of sacrifice I have made in practice, only known to Him, have brought me into a clearer, more complete reliance upon Him. The duty of confidentiality has uniquely sharpened my ability to play to a creative audience of One. I have found that having my focus squarely upon the quest to hear Him say 'you have done a beautiful thing' during such times of sacrifice enable His greater use of me into the future.

Though they may never be known in this temporal frame, our choices for washing the feet of our clients, joining in the beauty that Christ recognised in the woman's actions, will be revealed in eternity. The lawyer as creative plays to an audience of One. The Biblical promise is that our actions can align with beauty. We place our hope in Jesus' proclamation that what we have done is an objectively beautiful thing, in alignment, as καλός, with the nature of eternal beauty. Our service of our suffering clients, and our confidential experience of suffering in that service, present us Christian lawyers with a unique opportunity. We join in the experience of the woman with burial oil, in whose actions only Christ saw innate beauty. The distinct interplay of service and suffering offered by our vocation confers upon us a unique expression of the reality of objective beauty: beauty as sacrifice for the suffering with sole regard to the eternal audience of One.

## A Permanent Offering

I want to conclude this third lecture with this encouragement: in this mixture of service and suffering, by playing to an audience of One, the Christian lawyer makes a permanent, eternal offering. The question 'how are we to treat the natural human desire to leave a heritage within our work?' is a central theme of the book of Ecclesiastes. It presents a wealth of material for the lawyer that seeks to make the common good their life's work. The writer of Ecclesiastes (titled simply 'the Teacher') opens his book with the despairingly bleak assertion: 'No one remembers the former generations, and even those yet to come will not be remembered by those who follow them.'[230] Napoleon Bonaparte, a man whose life was driven by a morbid desire to leave a heritage, famously said 'there is no immortality but the memory that is left in the minds of men ... to have lived without glory, without leaving a trace of one's existence, is not to have lived at all.' Measured against the Biblical account, this is a decidedly anti-Christian idea. As the Teacher tells us in Ecclesiastes 4:4 'all toil and all achievement spring from one person's envy of another. This too is meaningless, a chasing after the wind.' Aware of pride (alongside *schadenfreude*) as a contender for the title of 'the besetting sin of the lawyer', we lawyers are in sore need of a conceptual framework that enables the healthy expression of the basic human desire to leave a heritage.

The Bible tells us that humanity has been 'created for God's glory'.[231] Humans were created with the need to give glory to God. John Calvin famously quipped that 'man's nature ... is a perpetual factory of idols'.[232] Disordered man not rightly related to God turns the human need to give glory onto himself. He fills the need to give glory by seeking to become the object of worship himself (the wrongly-directed need to give glory being not unlike one of Augustine's disordered loves[233]). In so doing he grapples to find the eternal, as Napoleon's life so powerfully evidences for us.

Much can be learnt on this theme from the writings and plays

---

[230] Ecclesiastes 1:11.

[231] Isaiah 43:7.

[232] John Calvin, *The Institutes of the Christian Religion*, tr Ford Lewis Battles (Westminister Press, 1960) 108, bk 1, ch 3.

[233] Augustine, 'City of God' (n 12) 416, bk 15, ch 22.

of Anton Chekov, where he made a perpetual study of the human desire for fame and to leave a legacy. In *The Seagull* Chekov explores these desires through the youthful Nina, who discovers to her shock that famous people are as engaged in trivial pursuits as are any of us:

> I used to think that famous people were proud and in-accessible and that they despised the crowd; I thought that the glory and lustre of their names enabled them, as it were, to revenge themselves on people who put high birth and wealth above everything else. But here they are, crying, and fishing, playing cards, laughing and getting angry like anyone else.[234]

However, although this discovery astounds her, it doesn't assuage or dull the lustre of fame for her. Later she concludes:

> For the sake of being happy like that - of being a writer or an actress - I would put up with unfriendliness from my family, with poverty and disappointment, with living in a garret and having nothing to eat but bread. I would gladly suffer dissatisfaction with myself in the knowledge of my own imperfections, but in return I would demand fame ... real, resounding fame.[235]

In Anya Reiss' interpretation, 'fame' here is interpreted as 'glory'. For Nina such troubles would be of no consequence, provided she attains to 'real glory'.[236] Notwithstanding her revelation as to the trivial pursuits of the famous, the elusive allure of 'glory' remains for her too great. As it turns out (spoiler alert) Nina does suffer all these things without achieving fame in her futile search for glory. In the short story 'First Class Passenger' Chekov has his protago-nist lament that his many efforts to achieve fame have failed on account of the base uncultured tastes of the masses, exclaiming in

---

[234] Anton Chekov, 'The Seagull', *Plays* (Penguin Books, 1959) 45, Act 2.
[235] Ibid 150.
[236] Anton Chekov, *The Seagull in a Revised Adaptation by Anya Reiss*, tr Anya Reiss (Bloomsbury Publishing, 2023) Act 2.

his despondency: 'if we knew what fame is, we might also know the ways of winning it'.[237] Both *The Seagull* and *The Cherry Orchard* focus on the insecurities of faded once-celebrities of the theatre, while *Uncle Vanya* explores the tragic tale of a middle-aged man who has spent his life futilely working to support the fame of another. Through many similar instances Chekov sheds light for us on the wretched state of those aspiring after the fickle recognition of other humans.

The writer of Ecclesiastes similarly grapples with the theme of the 'meaningless' desire to leave a legacy in the face of the futility of human toil, where 'all achievement spring from one person's envy of another'.[238] If there was no eternity, on its own, Ecclesiastes' Teacher's assessment that our 'lot' is that 'a man can do nothing better than to eat and drink and find satisfaction in his work' could appear as a cynical, devastating capitulation to the futility of temporal work.[239] But when Ecclesiastes is understood as presenting a contrast between the secular life of work without God, and a life in His service, we lose all fear that our work may be futile. Instead, our work takes upon a meaning that is imbued with God's purpose. The Teacher's assessment of our 'lot' is to be held up against the key hope pronounced in lecture 3, where the promise 'He has made everything beautiful in its time' falls immediately before the assurance that 'He has also set eternity in the hearts of men'.[240] The Bible's promise that everything will be made beautiful 'in its time' is not just for this temporal life, but also for eternity. It is the same hope Jesus expressed when the woman anointed Him with burial oil the day before His death – that which is objectively beautiful will prevail, even if we are the only ones who subjectively see it in the temporal world now.

---

[237] Anton Chekov, 'The First-Class Passenger', *Fifty-Two Stories*, tr Richard Pevear and Larissa Volokhonsky (Penguin Classics, 2020) 131.

[238] Ecclesiastes 4:4.

[239] Ecclesiastes 2:24, see also 5:18.

[240] Ecclesiastes 3:11.

## The Christian Lawyer and Beauty as καλός

I want to close with some reflections from NT Wright on the role of the Christian artist. I hope that you will recognise from what I have argued thus far that Wright's account of the Christian artist applies equally to the Christian lawyer or professional. Revelation 21:26 tells us that the new earth will commence as 'the glory and honor of the nations [are] brought into it.' As participants in that offering, we Christian lawyers will bring a unique and beautiful gift - our envisaging of the heavenly kingdom here on earth through works of justice inspired by Him as our creative acts of service. Seen as such, NT Wright's conception of the role of the Christian artist is equally true of the Christian lawyer. He writes:

> When art tries to speak of the new world, the final world, in terms only of the present world, it collapses into sentimentality; when it speaks of the present world only in terms of its shame and horror, it collapses into brutalism. The vocation of the artist [insert lawyer here] is to speak of the present as beautiful in itself but pointing beyond itself, to enable us to see both the glory that fills the earth and the glory that will flood it to overflowing, and to speak, within that, of the shame without ignoring the promise and of the promise without forgetting the shame.[241]

In the preceding lecture we discovered that injustice does not prevail against the true and prior ontology of peace, and that God's desire to direct 'the dawn … [to] take the earth by the edges and shake the wicked out of it' will be completed in the eschaton, where 'He will wipe every tear from' our eyes. It is this vision of justice that the Christian lawyer in her creative acts of beauty provides a window onto. The window onto justice she provides expresses to the world Christ's proclamation between the unity of subject and object. Just as the woman with burial oil produced a 'beautiful' work, so the

---

[241] Wright (n 22) 33.

lawyer's creative acts present a representation of the objective reality of peace as the true ontology.

The Christian lawyer is uniquely able, indeed burdened, to bring a vision of God's ultimate reality to those with a lived experience of injustice, those victims of evil on the steps of the court seeking justice. Wright continues: 'Here is the challenge, I believe, for the Christian artist [insert lawyer here] in whatever sphere: to tell the story of the new world so that people can taste it and want it, even while acknowledging the reality of the desert in which we presently live.'[242] In seeking to attain through our creative works to the objective reality of justice for our suffering clients we seek to tell the 'story of the new world'; that the true ontological reality is that of peace. So acting, the Christian lawyer invites her clients to subjectively appreciate that objective reality.

We have seen that Wolterstorff and Collingwood, in their focus on the artist's labour as an exercise in precise self-expression, imbibe the self-referential spirit of post-modern art critiqued by Gablik. The creative work of the lawyer, acquitting her duty of loyalty, provides a distinct rebuke to this conception. Her creative solution-finding efforts must remain other-focussed, expressive of her client's concerns. To this understanding the Christian lawyer adds a further question posed by CS Lewis (and one which also rebukes the self-referential spirit of modern art): 'Of every idea and of every method the Christian writer [or artist] will ask not "Is it mine?" but "Is it good?"'[243] The beautiful 'artifacts' of the Christian lawyer's creativity are works of justice, in alignment with the state of true eternal reality. Our creativity provides the proof of life that Solzhenitsyn hoped for when he asserted that 'the tops of these three trees' of 'Truth, Goodness and Beauty' may yet 'converge, as the sages said they did'.[244]

---

[242] Ibid.

[243] CS Lewis, 'Christianity and Literature', *Rehabilitations and Other Essays* (Oxford University Press, 1939) 195. I am indebted to Iain Benson for drawing this quote to my attention.

[244] Solzhenitsyn, 'Nobel Lecture in Literature 1970' (n 1) 13 (emphasis in original).

On this conception, Wright's vision of the artist applies equally to the lawyer:

> the present world is also designed for something which has not yet happened. It is like a violin waiting to be played: beautiful to look at, graceful to hold and yet if you'd never heard one in the hands of a musician, you wouldn't believe the new dimensions of beauty yet to be revealed. Perhaps art can show something of that, can glimpse the future possibilities pregnant within the present time.[245]

To continue to quote Wright, so conceived, the lawyer as 'artist is thus to be like the Israelite spies in the desert, bringing back fruit from the promised land to be tasted in advance.' In this vision the reality of suffering encounters God's directive to 'the dawn ... [to] take the earth by the edges and shake the wicked out of it'. Wright concludes:

> We are committed to describing the world not just as it should be, not just as it is, but as - by God's grace alone! - one day it will be. And we should never forget that when Jesus rose from the dead, as the paradigm, first example, and generating power of the whole new creation, the marks of the nails were not just visible on his hands and his feet. They were the way he was to be identified. When art comes to terms with both the wounds of the world and the promise of resurrection and learns how to express and respond to both at once, we will be on the way to a fresh vision, a fresh mission.[246]

I have developed a Biblical framework for action in which the lawyer performs the same role as what NT Wright conceives to be the role of the Christian artist. Who better to express the truth that eternal beauty entails justice than the Christian lawyer, positioned

---

[245] Wright (n 22) 35.
[246] Ibid 36-7.

as she is to respond to injustice, to create beauty in the face of suffering? In the Christian lawyer, so conceived, is fulfilled Solzhenitsyn's vision of the artist, with which these lectures opened: 'all that is given to the artist is to have a keener sense than others of the world's harmony and of the beauty and ugliness of man's contribution to it, and to convey this vividly to others.'[247] In this the Christian lawyer engages with what God chose to be the ultimate expression of His affinity with man: *suffering*. For it was by experiencing human suffering on the Cross that God ultimately set in motion the process that will bring to an end the suffering of humanity.

As Wright says '[a]rt at its best draws attention not only to the way things are but also to the way things will be, when the earth is filled with the knowledge of God as the waters cover the sea. ... perhaps it will be the artists who are best at conveying both the hope and the surprise.'[248] Let me go further in adding to Wright's hope and surprise, perhaps it will be the Christian lawyers who are best at *instantiating* in their service and in their own suffering that hope and that surprise. In seeking to align ourselves with the eternal form of beauty through our creative works, Christian lawyers, like Wright's vision of the Christian artist, model beauty in the face of suffering. This motivation for action applies equally to all those who serve the suffering within their chosen *métier*. In aligning ourselves with the καλός we are laying foundations of the eternal to come, for as Wright says, 'all of this will find its way, through the resurrecting power of God, into the new creation that God will one day make.'[249] Applying Wright's vision of the Christian artist to the Christian professional presents a theology sufficient to enable godly expression of the basic human desire to leave a heritage. It proceeds from the firm understanding that our acts of service and suffering will form part of the collective offering presented to Him on that final day; expressions of the objective reality of justice in alignment with what

---

[247] Solzhenitsyn, 'Nobel Lecture in Literature 1970' (n 1) 12.

[248] Wright (n 22) 37-8.

[249] Ibid 39.

He conceives to be beautiful. In the interim, this theology fit for a vocation looks to Jesus, as our audience of One, and the author of objective beauty, for pronouncement as to whether we may hold the subjective confidence that our creative efforts have indeed brought about 'a beautiful thing'.

## Lecture 3 Discussion Questions

1. Do you see your work as engaging in a creative process? If so, how? How would you describe your creative process?

2. In what ways does your work require collaborative creative efforts and how can you create further such opportunities?

3. To date, who has been the primary audience of your work?

4. Can you think of a matter in which having a firmer view of Christ as your audience may have changed the outcome? How so?

5. How can you express Christ's self-sacrificial love in your chosen profession?

6. Can your desire to serve Christ come into conflict with your obligations to your client, or those you serve, and how might you resolve this?

7. Without disclosing confidential information, have you ever had to keep a person's information confidential to your own detriment and how did you approach this? How can such experiences sharpen your resolve to play to the audience of One?

# LECTURE 4

## *Beauty and the Common Good*

### Our Present Moment

Thus far we have considered how beauty is related to justice and how it responds to the problem of evil. In light of this, we have developed an account of how the Christian lawyer and professional may present a picture of Christ's eternal beauty to the world through a single-minded focus on Him as the audience of our creative works. This has offered a theoretical framework sufficient to underpin our daily contributions to the common good. However, what remains is to consider whether there is a temporal end that we should desire as a result of the culmination of these many efforts? When we lawyers make our appearances in court or provide advice to our clients we may have a general awareness that our actions, as officers of the court, are contributing to the building of a just and ordered society. But do we ever take a moment to contemplate precisely how that just order might be best structured? That is to ask, do we professionals ever engage in the task of political philosophy? Given the effort expended in our daily actions toward the common good, we have a vested interest in considering not only the 'means' by which that good may be best attained, but also the precise content of the good we desire as an 'end'. In this final lecture I want to consider whether there is available to us a political philosophy that is attentive to the experience of the Christian lawyer, and which enables her unique calling to provide an account of objective beauty as God's desire for justice?

However, to consider our potential place in political philosophy we first need to attempt to understand the current prevailing political philosophy by which our society is structured – that of liberalism. In *On Poetics* Aristotle applied the term *mythos* (or 'Fable') to describe the plot within tragic plays, which he conceived as 'an imitation of an action', a *mimetic* representation of life.[250] John Milbank wants to apply the term *mythos* to liberal political philosophy in order to indicate his thesis (drawing upon Augustine) that liberalism presents a false theatrical narrative not truly representative of the true ontological ordering of human existence.[251] Whether we accept his thesis or not, his excoriating critique of the historical origins and presuppositions of liberalism invites us to a fresh awareness of our own limitations; that we are much like the proverbial goldfish to whom the question is posed: 'what is the water like?' and whose perplexed response is: 'what's water?' Thus, in making an attempt at a Christian political philosophy we do well to recall Sir Walter Scott's admonition that '[a] lawyer without history or literature is a mechanic, a mere working mason; if he possesses some knowledge of these, he may venture to call himself an architect.'[252]

To develop a political philosophy suitable to enable action by the Christian lawyer or professional we need to understand the *a priori* assumptions on which our current political order is founded, and in which we, like the goldfish, unknowingly swim. We need to interrogate those foundations if we are to develop an account that transcends those foundations. Why I say that we need to 'transcend those foundations' is because the Biblical account of the engagement between Christians and worldly authorities is a story that commences prior to liberalism and does not, of its own accord, offer reasons in support of liberalism's ascendancy. The Biblical account does, however, contain many themes that are of immediate relevance to the Christian who seeks a conceptual framework sufficient to enable just action within the state in which liberalism has assumed ascendency.

This task of developing such a Christian political philosophy

---

[250] Aristotle, 'On Poetics' in Robert Maynard Hutchins (ed), *Great Books of the Western World: Aristotle II*, tr Ingram Bywater (Encyclopaedia Brittanica, 1952) 684, ch 6.

[251] Milbank (n 43) 21-5, 55, 331, 374-5.

[252] Scott (n 194) ch 37.

is especially urgent to our time, for we sit at the end of an era – the end of the era that GK Chesterton called the 'Christian ideal'. When Chesterton said '[t]he Christian ideal has not been tried and found wanting. It has been found difficult; and left untried',[253] he was perhaps suggesting that the prior architects of Christendom misconceived both its proper means and its proper ends. He was also implying that 'the Christian ideal' continues to have relevance as a work of political philosophy. However, 114 years on from Chesterton's claim, we sit in a very different world. For many Christians the claim that our generation sits at the single greatest turning point in the history of the West since the conversion of Constantine in 312 AD no longer appears as hubris. So the question has arisen in the minds and through the actions of many Christian leaders, when is the use of earthly means justified for maintaining, or clawing back, our waning interests?

For many Christians the marked decline of Christianity was most notably signified by the legislating of same-sex marriage. In Australia the concern that same-sex marriage would unleash an assault on religious freedom saw many place great hope in the passage of religious discrimination legislation proposed by the former Morrison Government. It is my own reflection that the palpable, abject despondency of many Christians upon the defeat of that legislation in 2022 disclosed a distorted understanding of the relation of the Christian to the state. It reminded me of William T Cavanaugh's piercing insight into the besetting sin of the liberal state: the sin of state soteriology; the impulse of the liberal state to encourage its citizens to look to it for salvation.[254] The 2022 collapse of the near-on five year project to protect religious freedom through legislative means caused me to ask whether God was reminding us, in the words of the Psalmist, that '[i]t is better to take refuge in the Lord, than to trust in princes.'[255] Indeed, various Christian writers have

---

[253] GK Chesterton, *What's Wrong With The World* (Project Gutenberg, 1999) pt 1, ch 5.
[254] William T Cavanaugh, *Theopolitical Imagination* (T&T Clark, 2002).
[255] Psalm 118:9.

sought to remind us that when we look to a parliamentary democracy as the preserve of our freedoms we are effectively entrusting ourselves to a majority will, which may not be guided by Christian principles at all.[256]

It is against these challenges that Christian political philosophy must again show its utility. It must again mobilise its forces to provide an account that will guide Christians in their political engagement with the liberal democratic state. There are immense riches at our disposal. Christian political philosophy presents a tradition sourced from Augustine to Thomas Aquinas, through to Karl Barth and Reinhold Niebuhr in the twentieth century and the likes of Oliver O'Donovan and John Milbank in our own day. This final lecture is devoted to the search for a particular political philosophy that will sustain the Christian's response to these challenges. This task is urgent; Christians are grappling for the means to respond to these changes.

## Political Philosophy in Popular Culture

We again start our journey within contemporary popular culture. One need look no further than the success of the genre of mafia movies for proof of the human mind's fascination with the question of that which bestows legitimacy on a political order. Underpinning almost every mafia movie lies a question posed by Cicero in the first century BC, by Augustine in the fifth century AD, by Shakespeare in the seventeenth century and by John Rawls in the twentieth century: what confers legitimacy on power? In book IV, chapter IV of *The City of God*, Augustine states:

> that was an apt and true reply which was given to Alexander the Great by a pirate who had been seized. For when that king had asked the man what he meant by keeping hostile possession of the sea, he answered with bold pride, "What thou meanest by seizing the whole earth; but because I do it with a petty ship, I am called a

---

[256] See, eg, Stanley Hauerwas, *After Christendom?* (Abingdon Press, 1991); Patrick Deneen, *Why Liberalism Failed* (Yale University Press, 2018).

robber, while thou who dost it with a great fleet are styled emperor.[257]

From the very first moments of the seminal mafia film *The Godfather* we are offered an insight into an alternative account of power, one founded on absolute loyalty and on family obligation. Like Augustine's allegory of the pirate, *The Godfather* explores the legitimate, or illegitimate, use of violence. As we saw with Kelly Clarkson and Harry Styles in the first lecture, again popular culture engages with philosophy (here political philosophy) simply because philosophy deals with questions that are fascinating to the human mind. The appeal of mafia and gangster movies lies in their exploration of what is necessary for political order, and the question of when alternative authority structures may be legitimate. In so doing, they explore the necessary conditions for the exercise of legitimate human power. The distinction Augustine draws between the pirate and Alexander the Great explores the same theme. This leads us to the second great theme explored in mafia movies – the divide between loyalty to our collective and loyalty to the state. This theme is no less redolent for the Christian: when is our loyalty legitimately expressed toward the *civitas dei* (the heavenly city), and when is it legitimately extended toward the *civitas terrena* (the earthly city)? What are we to do in the event of a clash between the two loyalties?

## Political Philosophy in the Bible

If there is anything that the Bible conveys to us about human political ordering it is that it is a realm upon which humans place great expectations, but in which great peril resides. The warnings of the perils of trusting in human political authority start with the Israelites' call for a King; to which God responds you 'have rejected me as … king … you yourselves will become his slaves.'[258] The New Testament is replete with similarly low estimations of earthly political authority. Herod, despite his personal conviction that John the Baptist

---

[257] Augustine, 'City of God' (n 12) 190, bk 4, ch 4.
[258] 1 Samuel 8:7.

was a 'righteous and holy man' and despite being 'greatly distressed' at the request, capitulates and has John beheaded at the mere prospect of being shamed before his dinner guests.[259]

If anyone can attest to the fickle caprice of the crowd it is Jesus. His scepticism toward the crowd's call for miraculous signs sets the stage for the traverse from His welcome as a Saviour on Palm Sunday to His death the following Friday. His last sight is the mocking disdain and *schadenfreude* of the mob. Although 'knowing it was out of envy that the chief priests had handed Jesus over to him', Pilate, the embodiment of Roman *justitia* (justice) in first century Israel, cynically asks 'what is truth?' before sentencing to death a man he personally considered to be innocent. Mark tells us there was one simple motivation for this outrage against justice: Pilate's '[w]anting to satisfy the crowd'.[260] Above all else Pilate feared the disfavour of his overlords in Rome; the threat a rioting Jerusalem mob presented to his career. What a salient warning for the postmodern man who questions 'what is truth?' If there is a contemporary lesson to be taken from Pilate's example it is that postmodernism is the coward's option.

Mikhail Bulgakov offers a piercing insight into the significance of Pilate's encounter with Jesus for political philosophy in *The Master and Margarita*, written covertly during the Stalinist purges of the 1930s.[261] In Bulgakov's reimagining of the trial all that is necessary for Pilate to pronounce the death sentence against Bulgakov's Jesus (whom he renames Yeshua Ha-Nozri) is that he had the dismaying audacity to utter that the *pax romana* was not the final temporal authority, that another peace on earth would yet come. Perturbed and incredulous, Pilate's pleading that Ha-Nozri might take the effortless road of the recanter shows us the fear that haunts the political leader who is without any conviction as to 'what is truth'.

---

[259]  Mark 6:20.

[260]  Mark 15:15.

[261]  Mikhail Bulgakov, *The Master and Margarita*, tr Richard Pevear (Penguin Books, 1997).

The theme of the perils of trusting in human political authority is also seen in the book of Acts where Luke maintains a relentless critique. He tells us that all that was needed for Herod to arrest Peter was that James' execution 'met with approval among the Jews'.[262] In Corinth 'the crowd there turned on Sosthenes the synagogue leader and beat him in front of the proconsul' who 'showed no concern whatever'.[263] In the following chapter we are given the spectacle of the riot in Ephesus, provoked by the silversmith guild's concern that the sudden uptake of Christian belief would lead to a drop in the sale of their idols. Luke tells us the group that gathered in the town political 'theatre' 'was in confusion: Some were shouting one thing, some another. Most of the people did not even know why they were there', after which they broke into pagan chants that lasted for two hours.[264] Luke's retelling of the riot of the Ephesian silversmiths presents a most edifying study in the interface between human nature and political ordering. There is a consistent theme throughout these Biblical accounts: he who exercises political authority is always subject to the caprice of human nature, given most accurate collective expression in the inexplicable convulsions of the mob.

## Political Philosophy in Western Intellectual History

Warnings that we should proceed with caution given the dangers of human political ordering are not the sole preserve of theology. Such warnings are laced throughout Western political philosophy, and often make a particular focus on democratic orders. The following offers an illustrative, albeit brief, skim atop the waters of Western intellectual history. When Plato called *demokratia* a *theatrokratia* in *The Laws* he expressed the same concern reflected in the above Scriptures: the propensity of human political order to incline toward tyranny at the behest of the mob.[265] To illustrate this incline Plato sought

---

[262] Acts 12:3.

[263] Acts 18:17.

[264] Acts 19:32.

[265] Plato, 'The Laws' (n 20) 676, 701a. See also Plato, 'The Republic' (n 20) 427, 595b.

to draw out a parallel between art and political leadership: both are an imitation (*mimesis*) of an imitation of an unstable and uncertain understanding of reality. For Plato, both the tragic plays and democracy demonstrate that *mimetic* representation is always prone to morph into spectacle, and thus deception. The poets, in 'gathering crowds, and hiring fine, big and persuasive voices ... draw the regimes toward tyrannies and democracies'.[266] Plato's ultimate concern was that in giving rein to the baser sentiments, as does tragedy, democracy will descend into tyranny at the hands of the tyrant who promises to indulge the licentiousness of the people.[267] Critchley writes '[t]ragedy is the art form of tyranny that, through its very popular appeal and by *appearing* to satisfy the free desires of its spectators, enslaves citizens and turns them into subjects of spectacle'.[268]

The power of performative politics to hold sway over the crowd was also appreciated by Machiavelli, who considered the murder of Remirro by Cesare Borgia to be a brilliant public relations exercise: 'the ferocity of this spectacle left the people at once satisfied and stupefied'.[269] The awareness that political *mimesis* could become a tyrannical exercise in crowd manipulation flowed into liberal philosophy, where Rousseau, like Plato, banned the theatre from his Republic.[270] In *The Tragedy of Coriolanus* Shakespeare expresses the same insight into the interaction between the political leader and the crowd when he has an officer say:

> Faith, there had been many great men that have flattered the people, who ne'er loved them; and there be many that they have loved, they know not wherefore: so that, if they love they know not why, they hate upon no better a

---

[266] Plato, 'The Republic' (n 20) 415, 568c.

[267] Ibid 412-14, 562e-566e; 415, 568c; Strauss (n 18) 37.

[268] Critchley (n 162) 159 (emphasis in original).

[269] Niccolò Machiavelli, *The Prince*, tr Harvey C Mansfield (University of Chicago Press, 1985) ch 7 quoted in Manent, *An Intellectual History of Liberalism* (n 43) 19.

[270] Letter from Jean-Jacques Rousseau to D'Alembert, (1759) 159 quoted in Critchley (n 162) 42.

ground: therefore, for Coriolanus neither to care whether they love or hate him manifests the true knowledge he
has in their disposition; and out of his noble carelessness
lets them plainly see't.[271]

To the citizen's enquiry 'Was not this mockery?' Brutus replies with
a warning of Biblical proportion:

> He did solicit you in free contempt
> When he did need your loves, and do you think
> That his contempt shall not be bruising to you,
> When he hath power to crush?[272]

Closer to our own day, George Orwell draws upon similar wells
in *Shooting an Elephant,* his account of the traumatic experience of
being compelled to shoot an elephant by an urging crowd of locals
when a young official of the British Empire in Burma. Orwell's intent to build upon Western political philosophy's association of the
theatre with the crowd in this retelling is unmistakable. Orwell re-
counts that as he levelled his rifle at the beast he heard from behind
him the 'deep, low, happy sigh, as of people who see the theatre cur-
tain go up at last, breathed from innumerable throats'.[273] As a colo-
nial administrator he was 'seemingly the leading actor', 'but in reality … an absurd puppet pushed to and fro by the will' of the ruled,
for 'when the white man turns tyrant it is his own freedom that he
destroys'. Orwell's diagnosis was that 'it is the condition of his rule
that he shall spend his life in trying to impress the "natives", and so
in every crisis he has got to do what the "natives" expect of him'.[274]
On Plato's, Machiavelli's and Rousseau's view, Orwell's analysis of
'every white man's life in the East'[275] is equally applicable to political

---

[271] William Shakespeare, 'Coriolanus', *The Complete Works of William Shakespeare* (Rock Point, 2019) 978, Act 2, Scene 2.

[272] Ibid 982, Act 2, Scene 3.

[273] George Orwell, 'Shooting an Elephant', *Inside the Whale and Other Essays*
(Penguin Books, 1957) 97.

[274] Ibid 95.

[275] Ibid 96.

leaders within democracies. The relevance of the theme that political authority is ultimately at the mercy of capricious human nature is enhanced within democratic orders, where power ultimately resides in the majority. We encountered this thought in lecture 2 in WH Auden's poetic analysis of the law, *Law Like Love*. His depiction of the law as seen from the perspective of the democrat is:

> And always the very angry crowd,
>
> Very angry and very loud,
>
> Law is We,
>
> And always the soft idiot softly Me.[276]

As the protagonist in the episode of the slaughtered elephant, Orwell clearly conceived as himself as 'the soft idiot'.

## Political Philosophy in Augustine

Having heard these various theological and philosophical notes of caution, can we yet hope for a conceptual framework that will enable the lawyer to engage with the political in attainment of the common good? I want to commence the scoping of that account with Augustine. One of the central *leitmotifs* of Augustine's great tale of the two cities emphasises that, notwithstanding the Fall, it remains God's desire that Christians 'seek the peace and prosperity of the city'.[277] Notwithstanding the many theological and philosophical concerns with secular political power we have just encountered, Augustine would well agree with Victor Hugo's sentiment, expressed through the character Bishop Charles-Francois-Bienvenue Myriel, that '[i]t is wrong to become so absorbed in Divine Law that one is no longer aware of human law.'[278]

When considering the problem of theodicy in the second lecture we encountered Augustine's notion of the prior ontology of peace according to which God has laced throughout his creation certain

---

[276] Auden (n 184) 40.

[277] Jeremiah 29:7.

[278] Victor Hugo, *Les Misérables* (Penguin Books, 1976) 32.

default settings that bless all humanity. Augustine's assertion that these blessings continue despite the subsequent incursion of evil underpins his political philosophy. As Rowan Williams notes, 'we cannot say that [Augustine] has a theory of the state at all'.[279] However, we can say that his ontology of peace informs his conception of *radical* earthly institutions. For Augustine the precise form of the constitution is immaterial, provided it does not prohibit the worship of the citizens of the *civitas dei* while residents of the earthly city:

> This heavenly city, then, while it sojourns on earth, calls citizens out of all nations and gathers together a society of pilgrims of all languages, not scrupling about diversities in the manners, laws, and institutions whereby earthly peace is secured and maintained, but recognizing that, however various these are, they all tend to one and the same end of earthly peace. It therefore is so far from rescinding and abolishing these diversities, that it even preserves and adopts them, so long only as no hindrance to the worship of the one supreme and true God is thus introduced.[280]

Through the allegory of the pirate recounted above, Augustine intends to demonstrate that the defining feature of the state properly constituted is *justitia*. Notice what, for Augustine, that defining feature is not: it is not democratic accountability. Augustine's account of the role of the Christian in the state is decidedly jarring to Christians acclimatised to the power structures of the liberal state precisely because he poses no requirement that the Christian seek any particular form of political order. He expresses no particular preference between the three primary Aristotelian orders of democracy, monarchy or oligarchy.[281] Instead, his central theme is that of the sojourner, the Christian as a citizen of the *civitas dei* who exists, like Daniel, to bless the *civitas terrena* while resident within it, regardless of the form

---

[279] Rowan Williams, 'Politics and the Soul: A Reading of the City of God' (1987) 19/20 *Milltown Studies* 55, 58.

[280] Augustine, 'City of God' (n 12) 522, bk 19, ch 17.

[281] Aristotle, 'The Politics' (n 250) 475-477, 1278b6-1280a7.

it takes. Augustine's conception of the role of the religious believer within the state draws upon God's call in Jeremiah to 'seek the peace and prosperity of the city to which I have carried you into exile. Pray to the LORD for it, because if it prospers, you too will prosper'.[282] For Augustine, the question of the particular political structure that that state assumes is immaterial to the religious believer's role within it. His insight was fashioned according to the unique perspective he enjoyed: the dread of those (both non-Christian and Christian) living through the death throes of the Roman Empire.

Augustine is jarring to some contemporary Christian ears precisely due to his decided unwillingness to present endorsement to any particular political form. This reticence flows from his conception of Christians as citizens of the heavenly city, emplaced within an ontological and hence intellectual continuum that is external to the development of political philosophy within the West. This Augustinian perspective invites us to see how central is the assertion that our soteriology is not found in the state. Instead, the Christian's salvation lies in her identity as a citizen of a city resident within a continuum proceeding from an ontology of peace, and incomprehensible to the secular ordering of the *civitas terrena*.

This is a perspective that is at particular peril of being obscured for the resident of the liberal state. If Montesquieu and Rousseau are to be taken seriously, the liberal form of political ordering is founded upon the understanding that the state is our ultimate source of salvation and of virtue. How else could Rousseau assert that 'whoever refuses to obey the general will [being the collective reason as embodied in the legislature] shall be compelled to do so by the whole body. This means nothing less than that he will be forced to be free'?[283] That is, the liberal state will force acceptance of the reasoned outcome determined by parliament, and in that coercive act, the anti-liberal recalcitrant is set free. Similarly, Montesquieu's insight was

---

[282] Jeremiah 29:7.
[283] Jean-Jacques Rousseau, 'The Social Contract' in Ernest Rhys (ed), *The Social Contract and Discourses*, tr GDH Cole (Dent, JM, 1913) 18.

that the virtue proper to all republics is 'a renunciation of oneself ... [a] love of the laws and the homeland ... a continuous preference of the public interest over one's own, [which in turn] produces all the individual virtues'.[284] There, all private virtue stems from 'the love of the republic'.[285] 'Love of the homeland leads to goodness in mores, and goodness in mores leads to love of the homeland.'[286] Opposing moralities can be brooked only with suspicion in such a political order. It may be objected that this account of Montesquieu and Rousseau fails to offer a complete survey of the foundations of the contemporary liberal state, and that other more 'liberal' sentiments may be found within the writings of other founding liberal political philosophers. The ability of those alternative voices to prevail against Rousseau and Montesquieu's characterisation of the liberal state is a study that must be left to another day. It suffices for our current purposes to say that these liberal founders put us on notice of the need to apply strict scrutiny to the liberal state's willingness to permit alternative moralities and ontologies.

Notwithstanding that his focus on the citizen of the *civitas dei* as sojourner within the *civitas terrena* made him reticent to endorse any particular political form, a temporal political philosophy can be discerned within Augustine. It flows from his nascent notion of what we would now perhaps recognise as the doctrine of God's 'common grace'. Augustine conceived of the city as being comprised of certain rudimentary elements, including the *domus* and friendship, or associational endeavour. The *domus* and the *polis* each share in a form of common (and relational) peace:

> Since, then, the house ought to be the beginning or element of the city, and every beginning bears reference to some end of its own kind, and every element to the integrity of the whole of which it is an element, it follows plainly enough that domestic peace has a relation

---

[284] Charles Louis de Secondat Montesquieu, *The Spirit of the Laws* (Cambridge University Press, 1989) 35-6.

[285] Ibid 42.

[286] Ibid.

to civic peace—in other words, that the well-ordered concord of domestic obedience and domestic rule has a relation to the well-ordered concord of civic obedience and civic rule. And therefore it follows, further, that the father of the family ought to frame his domestic rule in accordance with the law of the city, so that the household may be in harmony with the civic order.[287]

For Augustine the peace of the *polis* flows from the prior peace of the *domus*. In a similar, way Augustine grounds associational freedom in the peace found between friends. That a form of radical peace is exhibited even between robbers united to a common purpose demonstrates how peace is both ontologically prior, and the rudiment of associational freedom.[288] In this Augustine refashions the classical notion of friendship away from Aristotle's magnanimous man and his denial that humans could ever be friends with the gods[289] to permit that 'friends'

> may mean those in the same house, such as a man's wife or children, or any other members of the household; or it can mean all those in the place where a man has his home, a city, for example, and a man's friends are thus his fellow-citizens; or it can extend to the whole world, and include the nations with whom a man is joined by membership of the human society; or even to the whole universe, "heaven and earth" as we term it, and to those whom the philosophers call gods, whom they hold to be a wise man's friends-— our more familiar name for them is "angels."[290]

For Augustine 'the whole use, then, of things temporal has a reference to this result of earthly peace in the earthly community, while in the city of God it is connected with eternal peace.'[291] Au-

---

[287] Augustine, 'City of God' (n 12) 522, bk 19, ch 16. See also 520, bk 19, ch 14.
[288] Ibid 517-19, bk 19, ch 12.
[289] Aristotle, 'Nicomachean Ethics' (n 250) bk 8.
[290] Augustine, 'City of God' (n 12) 510, bk 19, ch 3.
[291] Ibid 520, bk 19, ch 14.

gustine's political philosophy proceeds from the acknowledgement that our engagement with experience, with the whole (by some termed 'the absolute'), is through lived relationships and associative functions first and foremost. Augustine's preference for the bonds of immediate relationship as an outworking of the ontology of peace leads us away from the deracination that follows from viewing the citizen's individuality, her network of relationships, her lived experience solely through the prism of her relation to the state. However, Augustine's temporal political philosophy ultimately has its focus on the eschatological. In striving for 'the peace and prosperity of the city'[292] the citizens of the *civitas dei* seek to communicate to the *civitas terrena* the true ontology of eternal peace, which culminates in the heavenly city, but is modelled in their contemporary action.

## Tolstoy, Burke and Dostoyevsky in Raging Agreement

We are considering how we lawyers might acquit the Biblical charge to bless the postmodern society in which we find ourselves, while placing due weight upon the above theological and philosophical scepticism toward human political authority. Having thus far drawn upon Augustine's political philosophy in response to that challenge, I will complete my reply by marshalling the parallel insights of Count Leo Tolstoy, Edmund Burke and Fyodor Dostoyevsky. In *War and Peace* Tolstoy introduces us to Mikhail Speransky a real historical figure who for a brief period was a powerful liberal reformer enjoying the favour of Tsar Alexander in early nineteenth century Russia. Tolstoy's central protagonist Prince Andrei, a young, landed aristocrat, is enthralled by the brilliant Speransky and considers it the opportunity of his lifetime to draft legislation that would implement various of Speransky's leading liberal reforms. However, Prince Andrei's gradual process of disillusionment with the political process is brought to a climax when at a late-night dinner party he overhears Speransky jubilantly rejoicing in his own power and enlightenment while laughing with *schadenfreudistic* glee amongst his comrades

---

[292] Jeremiah 29:7.

at the plight of their misfortunate Russian subordinates. Disgusted, Prince Andrei immediately abandons Speransky's grand scale project of reform to return from St Petersburg to his remote estate there to implement his own liberalising reforms, including through the establishment of a school for the children of the estate's serfs.[293]

Through his reform efforts Speransky was channelling the utopian universalism characteristic of his time. Immanuel Kant gave expression to this universalism when he claimed that the upheavals of the French Revolution

> indirectly prepare the way for a great political body of the future, without precedent in the past … this encourages the hope that, after many revolutions, with all their transforming effects, the highest purpose of nature, a universal *cosmopolitan existence*, will at last be realised as the matrix within which all the original capacities of the human race may develop.[294]

For Kant:

> such a plan opens up the comforting prospect of a future in which we are shown from afar how the human race eventually works its way upward to a situation in which all the germs implanted by nature can be developed fully, and in which man's destiny can be fulfilled …[295]

On this basis Kant was ready to admit that 'philosophy too may have its chialistic expectations'.[296] (Chialism is the Christian belief in a coming millennium of global peace and harmony.) Again, at the foundations of liberalism we see clearly revealed the inclination toward state soteriology. Through Prince Andrei's engagement with

---

[293] Tolstoy (n 176) vol 2, pt 3, ch 18.

[294] Immanuel Kant, 'Idea for a Universal History with a Cosmopolitan Purpose' in Hans Reiss (ed), *Political Writings*, tr HB Nisbet (Cambridge University Press, 1970) 51 (emphasis in original). For a twentieth century articulation see WHG Armytage, *Sir Richard Gregory* (MacMillan, 1957).

[295] Kant, 'Idea for a Universal History with a Cosmopolitan Purpose' (n 294) 52.

[296] Ibid 50.

Speransky, Tolstoy is critiquing the liberal aspiration to universal-istic reform projects. Tolstoy warns us that grand scale projects of reform in the interests of an abstracted common humanity can be undertaken with a complete disdain for human nature. Echoing Augustine, he instead commends the bonds of personal relationship as the means by which lasting change is given effect.

In so doing Tolstoy offers to school us in one of the core tensions of political philosophy, the antinomy of the general and the particular, a tension which Deagon labels 'the very beginning of philosophy and theology.'[297] Aristotle considered the exchange between these two positions to be a problem that calls for perpetual reconciliation, as 'the general universal statement is inadequate insofar as it is indeterminate with respect to particular situations, while the more specific universal statement, though more determinate, is nevertheless liable to mislead.'[298] Edmund Burke exhorted a similar preference for the local over the abstract general in his excoriation of the universalising morality of the French Revolutionaries in *Reflections on the Revolution in France*. He critiques Jean-Jacques Rousseau the 'moral hero' of the Revolutionaries who

> constantly ... exhaust[ed] the stores of his powerful rhetoric in the expression of universal benevolence; whilst his heart was incapable of harbouring one spark of common parental affection. Benevolence to the whole species, and want of feeling for every individual with whom the professors come in contact, form the character of the new philosophy.[299]

Burke offers a simple cure to the human capacity for *schaden-freude* and hubris: we grow to love the whole by what we encounter in the particular. Also echoing Augustine, Burke famously conceived

---

[297] Alex Craig Deagon, 'The Contours of Truth' (PhD Thesis, Griffith University, 2015) 17-18.

[298] Daniel T Devereux, 'Particular and Universal in Aristotle's Conception of Practical Knowledge' (1986) 39(3) *The Review of Metaphysics* 483, 496.

[299] Edmund Burke, *Reflections on the Revolution in France* (Liberty Fund, 1999) 49.

of the 'little platoons' of family and associations as 'the first link in the series by which we proceed towards a love to our country and to mankind'.[300] Augustine, Tolstoy and Burke would all thus agree with the sentiment expressed at Proverbs 27:10, 'better a neighbour nearby than a relative far away'.[301]

Moving forward to the nineteenth century, drawing upon similar wells, almost fifty years before the Bolshevik Revolution Dostoyevsky warned of the potential for state imposed utopian visions to become totalitarian. In *The Devils* he analyses the psychology of the early Russian socialist movement of the mid-nineteenth century. He was well placed to offer such an insight, having been subjected to a mock execution on order of Tsar Nicholas I for being a member of a revolutionary cell in his youth. Through the character Shigalyov a subsequently enlightened Dostoyevsky dissects a political philosophy willing to sacrifice 'a hundred million heads' in order to achieve the 'future form of society right now'. In his enthusiasm Shigalyov unwittingly declares: 'Beginning with the idea of absolute freedom, I end with the idea of unlimited despotism'.[302] Dostoyevsky's answer (spoiler alert) to this augury of utopian brutality was as astounding for its simplicity as it was for its brilliance. Dostoyevsky concludes his seven-hundred page analysis with a simple unadorned account of the birth of a baby child. The reply to universalist utopian ambitions is a reaffirmed confidence in the timeless capacity of parental love as nature's (and thus God's) unsurpassed means to cherish the coming generation (what Augustine understood as the *domus*). This perhaps explicates the direct intellectual lineage coursing from Kant's philosophy to Stalin's dictatorship that Mikhail Bulgakov sought to illuminate when he has his chief protagonist proclaim in *The Master and Margarita*: 'your interlocutor [the devil] was at Pilate's, had breakfast with Kant and now he's visiting Moscow.'[303]

---

[300] Ibid 55.

[301] Proverbs 27:10.

[302] Fyodor Dostoevsky, *Devils*, tr Roger Cockrell (Alma Classics, 2017) 391, pt 2, ch 7.

[303] Bulgakov (n 261) 137.

Echoing Augustine, Tolstoy, Burke and Dostoyevsky all tell us that, if the challenge of politics is the resolution of the general to the particular, we must not seek a resolution that does not first proceed from a love of the particular. George Grant expressed a similar insight: 'We come to know and to love what is good by first meeting it in that which is our own - this particular body; this family, these friends, this woman, this part of the world; this set of traditions, this country, this civilisation'.[304] O'Donovan applies this reasoning to the task of political philosophy:

> We shall regenerate political thinking most effectively if we reflect upon the complex modes of human communication and privilege those patterns of giving and receiving which evidently meet the needs and satisfy those who participate in them and therefore contribute to forming community. [We have] the duty to be observant of human life before we rush in with our prescriptions for it; and to think *a posteriori* from lived experience of community rather than deductively and thus schematically and abstractly from above.[305]

As I argue in my PhD thesis, this understanding of political philosophy has consequence across various areas of the law, most notably the exceptions granted to associations within discrimination law, and the intervention of the state in the regulation of the civil society sector, including not-for-profits and charities.[306] Given human-

---

[304] George Grant, 'Technology and Empire' in Arthur Davis and Henry Roper (eds), *Collected Works of George Grant, vol 3, 1960-1969* (University of Toronto Press, 2005) 528. Thanks to Iain Benson for directing me to this delightful quote.

[305] Oliver O'Donovan, 'The Common Good: Does it Represent a Political Programme?', *Futures of Public Theology Conference, New College, University of Edinburgh*, (Centre for Theology and Public Issues, 01 December 2017) 08.40-09.31<https://youtu.be/vuTx6Z2jkzU>.

[306] Mark Fowler, 'Charity Law and Critiques of Modernity: An Application of Philosophical and Theological Critiques of Liberalism to Four Fields of Charity Law and Regulation: Civic-Engagement, Anti-Discrimination Law, Critique of Government Policy and Tax Exemption' (PhD Thesis, University of Queensland, 2023).

ity's basic Hobbesian desire for power[307] and its susceptibility to its Achilles heel of *schadenfreude*, the prudent course for engagement with politics is to eschew universalistic, chiliastic reform efforts and to instead seek to preserve and enhance a deep love of the personal, of the particular, when theorising society's structures of governance. Indeed, the success of our democratic system is in part owing to the fact that this understanding of human nature is baked into our political ordering. Electoral boundaries within our democracies are structured so to necessitate the love of the local. The future careers of all MPs within a democracy are dependent upon their ability to represent their local particular to the general view of the parliament. Tolstoy, Burke and Dostoyevsky all emphasise that in political ordering the general must be in service of the particular. Grand-scale efforts at political reform always risk injustice when they impose the general vision on the particular.

The Christian seeking to resolve this tension between the general and the particular in the political process may find a certain insight in Isaiah 57:15 where God says 'I live in a high and lofty place, but also with the one who is contrite and lowly in spirit'. This poetic phrasing suggests to us his singular potential, as Creator, to transcend the divide between particular and the general; that He alone offers the true hope of a resolution between the two. Despite that potential, the decline of religious faith and of local associational engagement within contemporary Western democracies has correlated with an increasing faith in political power, in the centralised state and in universal human rights.[308] Accompanying this development is an increasing willingness on the part of various interest groups to deploy centralised power to compel behaviour that is affirmative of their preferred worldview. In 1970, Solzhenitsyn recognised that postmodernism's denial of absolute truth traf-

---

[307] Thomas Hobbes, *Leviathan* (Penguin Books, 1968) 150; 161.
[308] Kerry O'Halloran, *Religion, Charity and Human Rights* (Cambridge University Press, 2014) 97-9.

ficked a corrosive message: 'you should always act exclusively in the interests of your own party' which, having been acted upon, has inspired a 'never-ending series of civil wars'.[309] Solzhenitsyn gives us an impassioned warning that

> the world is being flooded with the brazen assurance that might is omnipotent while right is powerless. Dostoevsky's *'possessed'* – figures, it would seem, in a fantastical provincial nightmare fantasy of a century ago – are swarming over the whole world before our very eyes and into countries which could not even imagine them before ...[310]

In the midst of this myriad of challenges, the Christian engaging in the political process within the postmodern liberal society does well to bear continually in mind that the human inclination toward power and susceptibility to *schadenfreude* will characterise politics; that only God is the source of the resolution of the general to the particular and that (contrary to the predilections of certain original liberal philosophers) salvation does not come from the state.

In this recap of what we have established thus far in our exploration of a Christian political philosophy, we thus return to the challenge of state soteriology. As I mentioned at the commencement of this final lecture, it is a challenge that the Morrison Government's failed religious reforms package brought squarely into view within Australia. For those Christians despondent at the collapse of the Morrison Government's efforts to protect religious freedom Augustine provides a prescient warning: 'earthly kingdoms are given by Him both to the good and the bad; lest his worshippers, still under the conduct of a very weak mind, should covet these gifts from Him as some great things.'[311] Of course, Augustine would not disavow the cry for legal protection for the victim of injustice. He

---

[309] Solzhenitsyn, 'Nobel Lecture in Literature 1970' (n 1) 19.

[310] Ibid 20.

[311] Augustine, 'City of God' (n 12) 206, bk 4, ch 33.

would however warn against placing our hope in state power at the expense of our expectation of Providence's intervention. The issue of state soteriology draws us to the final question I want to consider in this exploration of a political philosophy suitable to enable action by the Christian lawyer. It is a question of critical importance for those grappling with the end of Chesterton's 'Christian ideal': what role does God retain, if any, in political history? As I will argue, if there is any such ongoing role, this would directly challenge the notion of state soteriology.

## The Unseen Hand

Humans have long grappled with the question of the reality of Providential interference in human affairs. Sophocles' *Oedipus The King* is a study in the inexplicable. Oedipus' fall is a result of the direct interference of the gods in the *polis*. Sophocles does not seek to ameliorate the discomfort he leaves us with; the conclusion that the motives of the gods are inexplicable, that no matter the choices you make, fate will prevail. The Old Testament also presents a chronicle of the relations between a deity and humanity. It similarly accepts the thesis that the deity is directly involved in human political affairs. However, in contrast to Greek theatre, rather than humanity being the plaything of an inexplicable war between an incoherent gaggle of contesting gods, the Bible holds out the hope that the God that controls the universe is the 'I am', the single God in whom both mercy and justice cohere.[312]

The philosopher Leo Strauss argues that the question of God's interference in political affairs is deeply and uniquely problematic for liberal societies. His core charge against liberalism is that it is founded on 'secularization's' denial of Providence.[313] For Strauss the eschewal of the role of 'Providence' in the unfolding of history is a

---

[312] Exodus 3:14; 34:6-7.

[313] Leo Strauss, *Natural Right and History* (University of Chicago Press, 1953) 317; Seamus Deane, 'Burke in the United States' in David Dwan and Christopher Insole (eds), *The Cambridge Companion to Edmund Burke* (Cambridge University Press, 2012) 221-2.

core proposition of modernity's 'secularization' thesis.[314] On Strauss' thesis, liberal political philosophy and prophecy are in intractable competition. That competition can be seen as representing the contention between individual free will and divine determinism, expressed at the level of political ordering. To this debate Tolstoy's *War and Peace* adds a 1300 odd-page assertion that God's 'unseen hand' has not forsaken involvement in our history. Tolstoy's overarching theme is that, notwithstanding Speransky-style universalist and abstract liberal reform efforts, the hand of Providence remains the hand that continues to guide history. Tolstoy maintains that the rationale underpinning that hand is not revealed to us, it is inscrutable. Nevertheless, Tolstoy would surely affirm that, as Proverbs 25:2 tells us, it is 'the glory of God to be in the hidden, [while] It is the glory of a king to search out truth.' Even if God's ways may be inscrutable, the writer of Proverbs offers hope that our efforts in seeking out a Christian political philosophy, in 'searching out truth' are not then in vain.

## Can there be a Christian Political Philosophy?

So, can there be a Christian political philosophy? We have in light of recent Australian history highlighted the danger of seeing grand soteriological legislative schemes as the answer to the current challenges we might face; we have seen the Speransky solution is always at risk of jeopardy according to the human propensity for *schadenfreude* and our predilection for power. Echoing Augustine, Burke, Tolstoy and Dostoyevsky have counselled that we should seek the prevalence of the particular over the general, acknowledging that the general can be totalitarian where it prevails against the demands of the particular. Given we cannot downplay the role of the Providential hand, and understanding that that hand perfectly resolves the general to the particular, the key concern for the Christian engaged in the political process is: do we at all times allow that that hand may yet intervene? If we fail to admit of this, is it a sign

---

[314] Strauss, *Natural Right and History* (n 313) 316-23.

that we have accepted the counsel of certain early liberal philoso-phers toward state soteriology? The reality and inexplicability of evil in this world means that trite legislative solutions, the inor-dinate placing of our trust in political power, makes a mockery of God's Providence.

The current domestic tensions arising from the ructions in the Middle East provide a momentous test for cohesion within the po-litical project of Western democracy. However, we are not the first multicultural societies in which political philosophers have grap-pled with the means to assure social unity. In the last days of the Roman Republic Cicero theorised that a successful republic could be comprised by an assemblage of persons associated by common acknowledgement of certain rules for right and the pursuit of jus-tice.[315] Four centuries later Augustine critiqued that definition as in-adequate to the task of recognising and deepening the work of *cari-tas*. He offered a challenge in reply: the true republic is constituted by 'an assemblage of reasonable beings bound together by a common agreement as to the objects of their love.'[316] Despite his reticence to endorse any particular form of political ordering, Augustine does provide us with a schema for assessing political orders. Augustine's challenge to find 'common loves' founded in the common grace that God has laced throughout His creation remains as relevant to the project of political ordering today as it was in the last days of the Roman Empire. The current tensions refocus our attention on that age old question with a new urgency: what are the 'objects of love' sufficient to bind our society?

The Bible's counsel is that we won't attain to the final eschato-logical reality through earthly political order, despite Kant's great chiliastic hopes. However, with a sound grasp of this understand-ing, and by maintaining a keen awareness of the dangers of state

---

[315] Marcus Tullius Cicero, *Cicero: The Republic and the Laws* (Oxford University Press, 2016) 19.

[316] Augustine, 'City of God' (n 12) 528, bk 19, ch 24.

soteriology, our efforts toward the ordering of our society can be shaped by the eternal truth that God remains engaged in human history, and that, by proclaiming His authority, that history points to its ultimate culmination in eternal beauty. To the liberal society, Christians hold out the continuing hope of His Providence – His desire to order 'the dawn ... [to] take the earth by the edges and shake the wicked out of it'.[317] Against secular modernity we need to retain the expectation that God can intervene in history, while admitting that the state is not our saviour. Both admissions may well require us to challenge the founding precepts of certain liberal philosophers imbibed from the goldfish bowl we find ourselves currently swimming in. However, as Oliver O'Donovan writes, 'political criticism is not the deployment of a set of images to disclose a transcendent non-political reality; it is the expression of a hope for a real world under Christ's rule'.[318]

What then is the place of the Christian lawyer or professional within this political philosophy? Again, NT Wright's vision of the Christian artist's role in pointing to the beauty of God's eternal order is abundant with meaning:

> The resurrection of Jesus and the gift of the Spirit mean that we are called to bring forth real and effective signs of God's renewed creation even in the midst of our present age ... we are called to build for the kingdom. Like craftsmen working on a great cathedral, we have each been given instructions about the particular stone we are to spend our lives carving, without knowing or being able to guess where it will take its place within the grand design.[319]

I have sought to place before you a political philosophy that is accordant with a Biblical worldview. Rather than inspiring a with-

---

[317] Job 38:12-13.

[318] Oliver O'Donovan, 'History and Politics in the Book of Revelation' in Oliver O'Donovan and Joan Lockwood (eds), *Bonds of Imperfection: Christian Politics, Past and Present* (William B Eerdmans, 2004) 29.

[319] Wright (n 22) 34.

drawal into the catacombs,[320] it is a philosophy that invites the participation of the Christian lawyer who desires to make a contribution to the common good, to seek the prosperity of the society in which she finds herself. Like Augustine, it conceives of the citizen of the *civitas dei* as an agent of another world within the *civitas terrena*, a window disclosing a glimpse of the ultimate victory of peace. It takes up the hope that we identified in the third lecture on the Christian lawyer, beauty and creativity when searching through Ecclesiastes. Rather than our 'lot' being simply that 'a man can do nothing better than to eat and drink and find satisfaction in his work',[321] with the understanding that God remains at work in our present history, our work takes upon renewed meaning and repels all sense of futility.

## Conclusion

Let me attempt to draw these many threads together, which we have placed under the heading 'Beauty and the Law'. Our exploration of the relation between beauty and the law commenced with an overview of the intellectual history of 'beauty' within the West. We saw that the Kantian separation of subject from object culminated in the postmodern desire to 'thrash him' who asserts 'the true', 'the good and the beautiful are one'.[322] However, in charity and planning law's engagement with the aesthetic we found a willing declaration on the side of the unity of the subjective and objective. A similar conclusion was found in the law's Hegelian acceptance that beautiful artifacts can expose the 'uniqueness of a people ... which nothing else could have revealed to us.'[323]

In the second lecture we considered the relation of beauty to justice and its response to the problem of evil. We conceptualised

---

[320]  Rod Dreher, 'Orthodox Christians Must Now Learn to Live as Exiles in Our Own Country', 26 June 2016) <http://time.com/3938050/orthodox-christians-must-now-learn-to-live-as-exiles-in-our-own-country/>; Rod Dreher, *The Benedict Option* (Sentinel, 2018).

[321]  Ecclesiastes 2:24, see also 5:18.

[322]  Nietzsche, *The Will to Power* (n 58) 465, §822.

[323]  Malouf (n 83) quoted in Sheppard, Fitzgerald and Gonski (n 83) 182.

the common law adversarial system as a mechanism that harnesses postmodern insight to ultimately prevail against it. From these observations in philosophy and jurisprudence the third lecture landed upon a theological response to the Enlightenment denial of ultimate reality, the foundation of postmodernism. It is a response that Romantics like Wordsworth sought in these very Cumbrian hills; the reclamation of the unity between subject and object, but declared by the author of beauty, Christ Himself.

Building upon these various forays into the relation of beauty to the law, in the third lecture we developed an account of the Christian lawyer presenting a picture of Christ's eternal beauty to the temporal world through a single-minded focus on Him as the audience of her creative works. We found in the story of the woman with the anointing oil a declaration in defiance of Kant's proto-postmodernism, that that which is objectively beautiful is subjectively knowable. Beauty is what is determined by Jesus to be in coherence with what is eternally fitting and good. It was argued that this provided a fitting insight for the Christian lawyer seeking to give effect to God's vision of beauty as justice, to give effect to God's desire to shake injustice from this temporal world. As professionals, we seek His pronouncement of objective beauty, making it subjectively real to those in suffering that we serve. In so doing, we provide a window onto God's renewed creation, to adapt Wright, 'like craftsmen working on a great cathedral' whose beautiful final structure will ultimately be revealed for all to see in eternity.[324] The fourth lecture developed the argument that this *causa agendi* will be nourished by a political philosophy grounded in a realistic appraisal of the limitations and entrapments of secular political authority, in the preferment of local relationship over chiliastic reform efforts in the theorisation of society's governance structures (for 'better a neighbour nearby than a relative far away'[325]) and in a personal confidence in the ongoing role of Providence in defiance of modernity's exhortations toward state soteriology.

---

[324] Wright (n 22) 34.
[325] Proverbs 27:10.

In his Confessions Augustine laments his grief at not having come to faith earlier in his life, and in the years lost to his search for truth within false philosophies. He famously proclaims to God: 'Too late have I loved you, … Beauty of ancient days, yet ever new!'[326] God is eternal beauty. As Alpha and Omega, His beauty was present at the beginning and it will join with our created beauty at the end. While it is ancient, it is also ever new, ever ready to answer evil in our present day. We join the eternal continuum as the latest entrants into a community that is ontologically other; the long succession of those whose love for Him provides the foundation prior to the then ascendant political philosophy. Notwithstanding Nietzsche's claim that 'God is dead', [327]and regardless of the political framework in which they find themselves, the members of the *civitas dei* will continue their sojourn through the *civitas terrena* seeking its prosperity according to the true ontology of peace they instantiate,[328] persevering with the firm knowledge that the hand of Providence will prevail. Mark Twain's famous remark that 'reports of my death have been greatly exaggerated' might then equally be applied to Chesterton's 'Christian ideal'. For as Chesterton also wrote: 'Christianity has died many times and risen again, for it had a God who knew the way out of the grave.'[329]

---

[326]  Augustine, 'The Confessions' (n 129) 81, bk 10, ch 27.
[327]  Nietzsche, *The Gay Science* (n 105) 120, § 126.
[328]  Jeremiah 29:7.
[329]  GK Chesterton, *The Everlasting Man* (Hendrickson, 2007) 238.

# Lecture 4 Discussion Questions

1. Is it hubris to assert that we are living through an epoch defining moment?

2. When is it legitimate for Christians to seek political influence? How should they go about this?

3. Have you seen evidence that Christians are at risk of chiliastic political ambition?

4. How can we guard against this, while seeking to bless our society for Christ?

5. What contribution can you personally make as a Christian lawyer in response to these challenges?

# Bibliography

## Articles/ Books/ Reports

Abbott, Jo et al, 'The Impact of Loneliness on the Health and Wellbeing of Australians' (2018) 40(6) *InPsych*

Adorno, Theodore W, *Prisms*, tr Samuel Weber and Shierry Weber (MIT Press, 1967)

Angier, Tom, Iain T Benson and Mark D Retter, *The Cambridge Handbook of Natural Law and Human Rights* (Cambridge University Press, 2022)

Aristotle, 'Metaphysics' in Robert Maynard Hutchins (ed), *Great Books of the Western World: Aristotle I*, tr WD Ross (Encyclopaedia Brittanica, 1952)

Aristotle, 'Nicomachean Ethics' in Robert Maynard Hutchins (ed), *Great Books of the Western World: Aristotle II*, tr WD Ross (Encyclopaedia Brittanica, 1952)

Aristotle, 'On Poetics' in Robert Maynard Hutchins (ed), *Great Books of the Western World: Aristotle II*, tr Ingram Bywater (Encyclopaedia Brittanica, 1952)

Aristotle, 'The Politics' in Robert Maynard Hutchins (ed), *Great Books of the Western World: Aristotle II*, tr Benjamin Jowett (Encyclopaedia Brittanica, 1952)

Armytage, WHG, *Sir Richard Gregory* (MacMillan, 1957)

Auden, WH, 'Law Like Love' in James Fenton (ed), *The New Faber Book of Love Poems* (Faber and Faber, 2008)

Augustine, 'City of God' in Robert Maynard Hutchins (ed), *Great Books of the Western World: Augustine* (Encyclopaedia Brittanica, 1952)

Augustine, 'The Confessions' in Robert Maynard Hutchins (ed), *Great Books of the Western World: Augustine* (Encyclopaedia Brittanica, 1952)

Belmonte, Kevin, *The Quotable Chesterton: The Wit and Wisdom of GK Chesterton* (Thomas Nelson, 2011)

Betz, John R, *After Enlightenment: The Post-Secular Vision of JG Hamann* (Oxford Wiley-Blackwell, 2009)

BieMiller, Marc, 'Augustine and Plato: Clarifying Misconceptions' (2019) 29(2) *Aporia* 33

Blackburn, Simon, 'Collingwood, Robin George', *Concise Routledge Encyclopaedia of Philosophy* (Routledge, 2000)

Blake, William, 'And Did Those Feet' in Margaret Ferguson, Mary Jo Salter and Jon Stallworthy (eds), *The Norton Anthology of Poetry* (WW Norton, 5th ed, 2005)

Blond, Phillip, *Red Tory* (Faber and Faber, 2010)

Bolton, Geoffrey, *Edmund Barton* (Allen & Unwin, 2000)

Budd, Malcolm, 'Aesthetics', *Concise Routledge Encyclopedia of Philosophy* (Routledge, 2000)

Bulgakov, Mikhail, *The Master and Margarita*, tr Richard Pevear (Penguin Books, 1997)

Burke, Edmund, *Reflections on the Revolution in France* (Liberty Fund, 1999)

Cacioppo, John and William Patrick, *Loneliness* (WW Norton, 2008)

Calvin, John, *The Institutes of the Christian Religion*, tr Ford Lewis Battles (Westminister Press, 1960)

Cavanaugh, William T, *Theopolitical Imagination* (T&T Clark, 2002)

Chekov, Anton, 'The Seagull', *Plays* (Penguin Books, 1959)

Chekov, Anton, 'The First-Class Passenger', *Fifty-Two Stories*, tr Richard Pevear and Larissa Volokhonsky (Penguin Classics, 2020)

Chekov, Anton, *The Seagull in a Revised Adaptation by Anya Reiss*, tr Anya Reiss (Bloomsbury Publishing, 2023)

Chesterton, GK, *What's Wrong With The World* (Project Gutenberg, 1999)

Chesterton, GK, *The Everlasting Man* (Hendrickson, 2007)

Cicero, Marcus Tullius, *Cicero: The Republic and the Laws* (Oxford University Press, 2016)

Collingwood, RG, *The Principles of Art* (Clarendon Press, 1938)

Critchley, Simon, *Tragedy, the Greeks, and Us* (Pantheon, 2019)

Csikszentmihalyi, Mihaly, *Flow and the Foundations of Positive Psychology: The Collected Works of Mihaly Csikszentmihalyi* (Springer Netherlands, 2014)

Deane, Seamus, 'Burke in the United States' in David Dwan and Christopher Insole (eds), *The Cambridge Companion to Edmund Burke* (Cambridge University Press, 2012)

Deneen, Patrick, *Why Liberalism Failed* (Yale University Press, 2018)

Devereux, Daniel T, 'Particular and Universal in Aristotle's Conception of Practical Knowledge' (1986) 39(3) *The Review of Metaphysics* 483

Dickens, Charles, *Bleak House* (Electric Book Co, 2001)

Dickens, Charles, *The Old Curiosity Shop* (Open Road Media Integrated Media, 2015)

Dostoevsky, Fyodor, *Devils*, tr Roger Cockrell (Alma Classics, 2017)

Dostoyevsky, Fyodor, *The Brothers Karamazov*, tr David McDuff (Penguin Books, 1993)

Dreher, Rod, *The Benedict Option* (Sentinel, 2018)

Edelman, James, 'Original Constitutional Lessons: Marriage, Defence, Juries, and Aliens' (2021) 47(3) *Monash University Law Review* 1

Eliot, TS, 'The Love Song of J Alfred Prufrock', *Selected Poems* (Faber and Faber, 1954)

Eliot, TS, 'The Waste Land' in Margaret Ferguson, Mary Jo Salter and Jon Stallworthy (eds), *The Norton Anthology of Poetry* (WW Norton, 5th ed, 2005)

Eliot, TS, 'The Dry Salvages', *The Four Quartets* (Faber & Faber, 2019)

Eliot, TS, 'East Coker', *The Four Quartets* (Faber & Faber, 2019)

Ermath, Elizabeth, 'Postmodernism', *Concise Routledge Encyclopaedia of Philosophy* (Routledge, 2000)

Finnis, John, *Natural Law and Natural Rights* (Oxford University Press, 2nd ed, 2011)

Gablik, Suzi, *Has Modernism Failed?* (Thames and Hudson, 1984)

Gallant, James, 'What am I Doing?' (2023) 153 *Philosophy Now* 19

Galovic, Michael, *Sailing Back to Byzantium* (Yarra & Hunter Arts Press, 2024)

Grant, George, *English-Speaking Justice* (University of Notre Dame Press, 1985)

Grant, George, 'Technology and Empire' in Arthur Davis and Henry Roper (eds), *Collected Works of George Grant, vol 3, 1960-1969* (University of Toronto Press, 2005)

Hamann, Johann Georg, in Josef Nadler (ed), *Sämtliche Werke* (Herder, 1949-57)

Hamann, Johann Georg, *Writings on Philosophy and Language*, tr Kenneth Haynes (Cambridge University Press, 2007)

Hauerwas, Stanley, *After Christendom?* (Abingdon Press, 1991)

Hegel, GWF, *Aesthetics: Lectures on Fine Art*, tr TM Knox (Clarendon, 1975)

Hobbes, Thomas, *Leviathan* (Penguin Books, 1968)

*The Holy Bible: New International Version*, (Biblica, 2011)

*The Holy Bible: The Passion Translation* (Broadstreet Publishing Group, 2020) https://www.thepassiontranslation.com/read-online/

Honderich, Ted, *Oxford Companion to Philosophy* (Oxford University Press, 1995)

Hugo, Victor, *Les Misérables* (Penguin Books, 1976)

Hume, David, *A Treatise of Human Nature* (Clarendon Press, 1896)

Hume, David, *An Enquiry Concerning Human Understanding* (Clarendon Press, 1902)

Jones, Les, 'Plaiting Gravy' (2023) 153 *Philosophy Now* 8

Judge, Edwin, *Jerusalem and Athens* (Mohr Siebeck, 2010)

Kant, Immanuel, 'The Critique of Judgement' in Robert Maynard Hutchins (ed), *Great Books of the Western World: Kant* tr James Creed Meredith (Encyclopaedia Brittannica, 1952)

Kant, Immanuel, 'The Critique of Pure Reason', in Robert Maynard Hutchins (ed), *Great Books of the Western World: Kant* tr JMD Meiklejohn (Encyclopedia Brittannica, 1952).

Kant, Immanuel, 'Idea for a Universal History with a Cosmopolitan Purpose' in Hans Reiss (ed), *Political Writings*, tr HB Nisbet (Cambridge University Press, 1970)

Keats, John, 'Endymion', *The Complete Poems of Shelley and Keats* (Random House, 1978)

Keats, John, 'Lamia', *The Complete Poems of Shelley and Keats* (Random House, 1978)

Keats, John, 'Ode On a Grecian Urn', *The Complete Poems of Shelley and Keats* (Random House, 1978)

Kenney, John Peter, '"None Come Closer to Us than These:" Augustine and the Platonists' (2016) 7(9) *Religions* 114

La Nauze, JA, *The Making of the Australian Constitution* (Melbourne University Press, 1972)

Lennox, John C, *Against the Flow* (Monarch Books, 2015)

Lewis, CS, 'Christianity and Literature', *Rehabilitations and Other Essays* (Oxford University Press, 1939)

Lewis, CS, *The Abolition of Man* (The Macmillan Company, 1947)

Lewis, CS, *The Weight of Glory and Other Addresses* (The Macmillan Company, 1949)

Lewis, CS, *Mere Christianity* (Pomodoro Books, 2020)

Machiavelli, Niccolò, *The Prince*, tr Harvey C Mansfield (University of Chicago Press, 1985)

Mahoney, Daniel J, 'Communion and Consent' (2012) 41(2) *Perspectives on Political Science* 93

Maistre, Joseph de, *St Petersburg Dialogues*, tr Richard Lebrun (McGill-Queen's University Press, 1993)

Manent, Pierre, *An Intellectual History of Liberalism*, tr Rebecca Balinksi (Princeton University Press, 1995)

Manent, Pierre, *The City of Man*, tr Marc A LePain (Princeton University Press, 1998)

Milbank, John, *Theology and Social Theory* (Blackwell Publishing, 2nd ed, 2006)

Montesquieu, Charles Louis de Secondat, *The Spirit of the Laws* (Cambridge University Press, 1989)

Mulligan, Jina, 'The Timeless Dance: A Sacred Work of Art by Michael Galovich', *Sailing Back to Byzantium* (Yarra & Hunter Arts Press, 2024)

Myers, Andrew, '03 January Looking Forward to the Year Ahead', *Faithful and Fruitful: 365 Daily Devotions Written by Lawyers for Lawyers* (The Lawyers' Christian Fellowship, 2023)

Nietzsche, Friedrich, *Ecce Homo*, tr Anthony M Ludovici (TN Foulis, 1911)

Nietzsche, Friedrich, *Thus Spoke Zarathustra*, tr RJ Hollingdale (Penguin Books, 1961)

Nietzsche, Friedrich, *Beyond Good and Evil*, tr Walter Kaufmann (Vintage Books, 1966)

Nietzsche, Friedrich, *The Gay Science*, tr Josefine Nauckhoff and Adrian Del Caro (Cambridge University Press, 2001)

Nietzsche, Friedrich, *The Genealogy of Morals*, tr Horace B Samuel (Dover Publications Inc, 2003)

Nietzsche, Friedrich, *Twilight of the Idols and The Anti-Christ*, tr RJ Hollingdale (Penguin, 2003)

Nietzsche, Friedrich, *The Will to Power*, tr R Kevin Hill and Michael A Scarpatti (Penguin Books, 2017)

O'Donovan, Oliver, 'History and Politics in the Book of Revelation' in Oliver O'Donovan and Joan Lockwood (eds), *Bonds of Imperfection: Christian Politics, Past and Present* (William B Eerdmans, 2004)

O'Donovan, Oliver, *The Ways of Judgement* (William B Eerdmans, 2005)

O'Halloran, Kerry, *Religion, Charity and Human Rights* (Cambridge University Press, 2014)

Orwell, George, 'Shooting an Elephant', *Inside the Whale and Other Essays* (Penguin Books, 1957)

Plato, 'The Laws' in Robert Maynard Hutchins (ed), *Great Books of the Western World: The Dialogues of Plato* tr Benjamin Jowett (Encyclopaedia Brittanica, 1952)

Plato, 'The Republic' in Robert Maynard Hutchins (ed), *Great Books of the Western World: The Dialogues of Plato*, tr Benjamin Jowett (Encyclopaedia Brittanica, 1952)

Plato, 'Symposium' in Robert Maynard Hutchins (ed), *Great Books of the Western World: The Dialogues of Plato*, tr Benjamin Jowett (Encyclopaedia Brittanica, 1952)

Plato, 'Theaetetus' in Robert Maynard Hutchins (ed), *Great Books of the Western World: The Dialogues of Plato*, tr Benjamin Jowett (Encyclopaedia Brittanica, 1952)

Ranieri, John, 'Leo Strauss on Jerusalem and Athens' (2002) 22(2) *Shofar* 85

Rawls, John, *A Theory of Justice* (Belknap Press, rev ed, 1999)

Rousseau, Jean-Jacques, 'The Social Contract' in Ernest Rhys (ed), *The Social Contract and Discourses*, tr GDH Cole (Dent, JM, 1913)

Scarry, Elaine, *On Beauty and Being Just* (Princeton University Press, 1999)

Scott, Walter, *Guy Mannering* (EP Dutton & Company, 1908)

Scruton, Roger, *The Face of God: The Gifford Lectures* (Bloomsbury Publishing Plc, 2014)

Shakespeare, William, 'Henry VI', *The Complete Works of William Shakespeare* (Rock Point, 2014)

Shakespeare, William, 'Coriolanus', *The Complete Works of William Shakespeare* (Rock Point, 2019)

Sheppard, I, R Fitzgerald and D Gonski (Commonwealth of Australia), *Report of the Inquiry into the Definition of Charities and Related Organisations*, 28 June 2001)

Smith, James KA, *On the Road with Saint Augustine* (Brazos Press, 2019)

Solzhenitsyn, Aleksandr, *The Gulag Archipelago* (Collins, 1974)

Strauss, Leo, *Natural Right and History* (University of Chicago Press, 1953)

Strauss, Leo, 'Progress or Return?' (1981) 1(1) *Modern Judaism* 17

Taylor, Charles, *A Secular Age* (Harvard University Press, 2007)

Tertullian, 'De Praescriptione Haereticorum' 7(34)

Til, Kent van, 'Subsidiarity and Sphere-Sovereignty' (2008) 69 *Theological Studies* 610

Tolstoy, Leo, *War and Peace*, tr Richard Pevear and Larissa Volokhonsky (Vintage Classics, 2009)

Torke, James W, 'The Aesthetics of Law' (2003) 48 *American Journal of Jurisprudence* 325

Weil, Simone, *A Cabinet of Curiosities: Inquiries into Museums and their Prospects* (Smithsonian Institute Press, 1995)

Williams, Rowan, 'Politics and the Soul: A Reading of the City of God' (1987) 19/20 *Milltown Studies* 55

Wise, Bernhard Ringrose, *The Making of the Australian Commonwealth 1889-1900: A Stage in the Growth of the Empire* (Longmans, Green, and Co, 1913)

Wolterstorff, Nicholas, 'Beauty and Justice' (2009) 73(4) *The Cresset* 6

Wood Jr, John Halsey, 'Unity and Engagement in the Modern World: Abraham Kuyper's Calvinist Renewal' in Bruce Gordon and Carl R Trueman (eds), *The Oxford Handbook of Calvin and Calvinism* (Oxford University Press, 2021) 508

Wordsworth, Dorothy, *Recollections of a Tour Made in Scotland, 1803* (Yale University Press, 1997)

Wordsworth, William, 'It Is a Beauteous Evening' in Margaret Ferguson, Mary Jo Salter and Jon Stallworthy (eds), *The Norton Anthology of Poetry* (WW Norton, 5th ed, 2005)

Wreen, Michael, 'Collingwood, Robin George' in Ted Honderich (ed), *Oxford Companion to Philosophy* (Oxford University Press, 1995)

Wright, NT, *On Earth as in Heaven* (HarperOne, 2022)

## Cases

*Commissioners of Inland Revenue v White* (1980) 55 TC 651

*Re Chanter (deceased)* [1952] SASR 299

*Re Perpetual Trustees Queensland Ltd* [2000] 2 Qd R 647

*Re Pinion (deceased)* [1964] 1 All ER 890

*Re Shaw's Will Trusts* [1952] 1 Ch 163

*Royal Choral Society v Commissioners of Inland Revenue* [1943] 2 All ER 101

## Other

'Bell Shakespeare Enlists Robert Menzies for Titular King Lear Role', *RN Breakfast*, (ABC Radio National, 09 June 2024) https://www.abc.net.au/listen/programs/radionational-breakfast/king-lear-bell-shakespeare/103932836

Benson, Iain T, 'The Relationship Between Beauty and Justice' (Lecture, Roundtable for the Western Heritage Association, 21 February 2023)

Bradley, Thomas, 'Legal History and Human Rights - Reflections on the Revolution' (Lecture, Sir Samuel Griffith Society 34th Conference, 25 May 2024)

British Broadcasting Corporation, *Why Beauty Matters* (British Broadcasting Corporation, 2009)

Building Better Building Beautiful Commission, 'Living with Beauty: Promoting Health, Well-Being and Sustainable Growth' (Report, January 2020) <https://assets.publishing.service.gov.uk/media/5e3191a9ed915d0938933263/Living_with_beauty_BBBBC_report.pdf>

Deagon, Alex Craig, 'The Contours of Truth' (PhD Thesis, Griffith University, 2015)

Department for Digital Culture Media and Sport, *A Connected Society*, (October 2018)

Department for Levelling Up Housing & Communities, 'Decision on Correction Notice under Section 57 of the Planning and Compulsory Purchase Act 2004, Application made by MEC London Property 3 (General Partner) Limited regarding former London Television Centre, 60-72 Upper Ground, London, SE1 9LT' (Application Ref: 21/02668/EIAFUL, (Decision Officer Stasiak), 09 February 2024)

Dreher, Rod, 'Orthodox Christians Must Now Learn to Live as Exiles in Our Own Country', 26 June 2016) <http://time.com/3938050/orthodox-christians-must-now-learn-to-live-as-exiles-in-our-own-country/>

Fowler, Mark, 'Charity Law and Critiques of Modernity: An Application of Philosophical and Theological Critiques of Liberalism to Four Fields of Charity Law and Regulation: Civic-Engagement, Anti-Discrimination Law, Critique of Government Policy and Tax Exemption' (PhD Thesis, University of Queensland, 2023)

George, Gav 'Rise of the Law-medians: Lawyers Drop Out to Become Comedians', *enhancentertainment* <https://enhancentertainment.com.au/blog/rise-of-law-medians-lawyers-drop-out-become-comedians/>.

Malouf, David, 'Foreword', *Securing our Future: Major Performing Arts Inquiry* (Discussion Paper, July 1999)

Ministry of Housing Communities and Local Government, 'National Planning Policy Framework', (December 2023) <https://assets.publishing.service.gov.uk/media/669a25e9a3c2a28abb50d2b4/NPPF_December_2023.pdf>

New South Wales Parliament Standing Committee on Social Issues, 'Prevalence, Causes and Impacts of Loneliness in New South Wales', *parliament.nsw.gov.au* (Web Page, 06 August 2024) <https://www.parliament.nsw.gov.au/committees/inquiries/Pages/inquiry-details.aspx?pk=3066>

O'Donovan, Oliver, 'The Common Good: Does it Represent a Political Programme?', *Futures of Public Theology Conference, New College, University of Edinburgh*, (Centre for Theology and Public Issues, 01 December 2017) <https://youtu.be/vuTx6Z2jkzU>

Prime Minister's Office, 'PM Launches Government's First Loneliness Strategy', *gov.uk* (Press Release, 16 October 2018) <https://www.gov.uk/government/news/pm-launches-governments-first-loneliness-strategy>

Rousseau, Jean-Jacques, letter to D'Alembert', (1759)

Solzhenitsyn, Aleksandr, 'Nobel Lecture in Literature 1970' *Letter to The Swedish Academy*, 1970, tr Michael Scammell 12 <https://journals.sagepub.com/doi/pdf/10.1177/030642207200103-402>

# Index

# Index of Scripture References

# ABOUT THE AUTHOR

Husband to Sarah and father to Caitlyn and Ethan, Dr Mark Fowler is a practising lawyer and Principal of Fowler Charity Law. He is Chair of the Australian Christian Legal Society Ltd and an Adjunct Associate Professor both at the University of Notre Dame, School of Law, Sydney, and the Law School at his *alma mater*, the University of New England. He is also an External Fellow at the Centre for Public, International and Comparative Law, University of Queensland, where he was awarded his doctorate in 2023. His legal practice focusses upon the law applying to schools, international aid organisations, arts and cultural organisations and religious organisations. He is an Appeals Panel member for the Australian Council for International Development (ACFID), the peak body for Australian non-government organisations involved in international development and humanitarian action. He is a member of the Australian Charities and Not-for-Profits Commission Professional Users Group and has served as a member of the Queensland Law Society's Human Rights Working Group.

www.ingramcontent.com/pod-product-compliance
Lightning Source LLC
Chambersburg PA
CBHW061254220326
41599CB00028B/5642